East Asian History

1000 Fascinating Facts About China and Japan

Welcome Aboard, Check Out This Limited-Time Free Bonus!

Ahoy, reader! Welcome to the Ahoy Publications family, and thanks for snagging a copy of this book! Since you've chosen to join us on this journey, we'd like to offer you something special.

Check out the link below for a FREE e-book filled with delightful facts about American History.

But that's not all - you'll also have access to our exclusive email list with even more free e-books and insider knowledge. Well, what are ye waiting for? Click the link below to join and set sail toward exciting adventures in American History.

Access your bonus here: https://ahoypublications.com/

Or, Scan the QR code!

Table of Contents

Part 1: Chinese History
500 Interesting Facts About China

Introduction

For generations, **the history of China has been a story filled with success and struggle.** From pre-imperial China to the People's Republic of China, Chinese civilization has experienced astounding accomplishments and grave challenges.

This book provides an overview of the notable periods in Chinese history, from **the Qin dynasty** to **China's Open Door Policy**. In each chapter, we will explore the cultural and political landscape of China through dynasties like **the Han** and **Southern Song** and through tumultuous events like **the Opium Wars** and **the Taiping Rebellion.**

We will also examine some of **the pivotal moments in modern Chinese history**, including **Yuan Shikai's** attempt to reestablish imperial rule, **the Chinese Civil War, the Cultural Revolution, the Tiananmen Square protests**, and the rise of China as a superpower. Throughout this book, we will take a close look at notable milestones and small details that give insight into how these periods shaped modern culture.

By reading about history, we gain a better understanding of cultures and modern-day events. **This is an adventure into the past** that will not only enlighten us but also captivate our imaginations and leave us eager to explore even more.

Pre-Imperial China
(ca. 2000–221 BCE)

This chapter will explore the fascinating history of pre-imperial China with thirty interesting facts. With this insight into pre-imperial Chinese society, we can gain a greater appreciation for its sophistication and resilience during this time in history.

1. **Pre-imperial China** lasted from about 2000 BCE to 221 BCE.
2. During this time, **the Chinese people spoke many different languages** and followed different customs, depending on where they lived in China.
3. The dominant group during pre-imperial times was **the Zhou dynasty** (1046–256 BCE).
4. **The Chinese developed complex systems of government**, law, and writing that lasted for centuries after the pre-imperial period ended.
5. **Pre-imperial Chinese society was split into classes** based on wealth, power, and ancestry.
6. **Farmers provided food to feed everyone**. Millet was one of the most important crops in ancient China.

7. Effectively **managing water resources became an integral part of daily life** due to the frequent flooding of nearby rivers. With the help of wealthy landlords, who often owned large tracts of land alongside rivers, **the Chinese** were able to build irrigation systems.

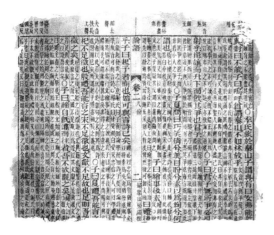

8. **Confucius was a famous Chinese philosopher** who lived during pre-imperial times. His teachings on morality, justice, and respect were highly influential in imperial China. They still continue to shape Chinese society to a large degree today.
9. During this period, **some of the earliest forms of martial arts emerged**. Probably dating back to **the Xia dynasty about four thousand years ago**, the main use of martial arts was for self-defense and hunting.

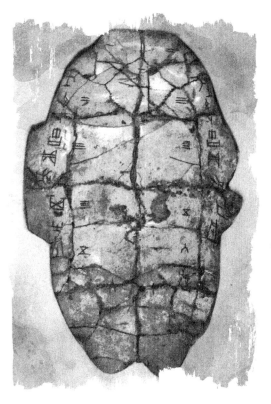

10. **The Silk Road was an overland trade route connecting Asia to Europe.** It had multiple routes that ran **from China through central Asia to the West.** While evidence of trade via **the Silk Road** during pre-imperial times has been discovered in various parts of Eurasia, the trade route would become far more cohesive in the 2nd century BCE.

11. **The earliest Chinese writing comes from the pre-imperial era.** A pictographic script known as *jiaguwen* **has been found on animal bones and turtle shells** dating back to about 1200 BCE.

12. Objects from **early Bronze Age tombs reveal that people knew astronomy and mathematics.** Archeologists have discovered lacquer boxes containing names of tens of lunar mansions (divisions of the sky), dating back to the 5th century BCE.

13. **The construction of walls that later joined to form the Great Wall started in the 7th century BCE.** The walls were meant to defend the Chinese lands from northern invaders. They were built partially from stone, wood, and rammed earth.

14. **Different sections of the Great Wall were added throughout the centuries.** The final sections of the wall were completed during **the Ming dynasty (1368–1644 CE),** meaning that it took more than **two thousand years to finish the Great Wall!**

15. **Chinese invented primitive compasses** around the 4th century BCE. These compasses weren't used to find the way north. **They were used to find the right direction in life.** These compasses were **used in rituals, feng shui practices, and fortune-telling.**

16. **Philosophical schools** of thought such as **Daoism, Confucianism, and Mohism** heavily influenced pre-imperial China.

17. **Ancient Chinese believed in ancestor worship**. They would honor their ancestors with offerings of food or incense placed on altars.

18. **Bronze vessels and weapons were common during pre-imperial times**. These objects often had intricate designs etched into them.

19. The earliest coins developed in East Asia came from the Zhou dynasty (1046–256

BCE). However, no developed monetary system existed, and the coins did not look like the coins we use today. Instead, things found in nature, like cowrie shells, were frequently used.

20. An interesting discovery dating back to pre-imperial China is oracle bones. Bones were inscribed with important questions on weather or battles and then were heated up until they produced cracks. **The patterns provided by the cracks were then interpreted by oracles.**

21. Tea drinking became popular in parts of China during the Zhou dynasty. Although it was **first used for medicinal purposes**, the nobility started to pick up tea drinking as a luxury activity.

22. Ancient Chinese people developed some of the earliest forms of pottery and ceramics. They used these items for cooking, storage, and burial.

23. Traditional Chinese medicine has been practiced since pre-imperial times. Healers would use herbs and acupuncture techniques to treat illnesses.

24. Thought to exist from around 2000 to 1600 BCE, the semi-mythical Xia dynasty is considered to be one of the first (if not the first) **ruling dynasties of ancient China.** It is commonly held that the first Xia ruler by the name of Yu was the first to obtain the divine right to rule, also known as the Mandate of Heaven.

25. Pre-imperial China saw an exceptional advancement in metallurgy. Iron tools and weapons slowly replaced bronze toward the end of the 6th century BCE in the Yangtse Valley. Iron would become the preferred metal of choice around 300 BCE.

26. **Perhaps the most famous piece of literature written during the pre-imperial era is *The Art of War* by military strategist Sun Tzu.** The book was written sometime in the 5th century BCE and remains a popular military treatise to this day.

27. Other classics, like **the late 9th-century BCE *I Ching*** (*Book of Changes*) and **the 5th-century BCE *Tao Te Ching*** (*Book of the Way*), were also composed during this era.

28. **One of the most fundamental ideas of ancient Chinese culture is yin and yang, a concept that states everything has two opposite yet interconnected sides.** Although these terms weren't used in the pre-imperial era, there is evidence that the idea behind yin and yang was starting to form.

29. **The pre-imperial era saw the first few iterations of Chinese calendars.** The ancient Chinese used solar calendars. **During the Zhou dynasty, the Chinese used a lunisolar calendar.**

30. **Pre-imperial China saw exceptional advances in mathematics**. They developed math independently (meaning they weren't influenced by other civilizations) during the 11th century BCE.

Qin Dynasty
(221–206 BCE)

Discover the fascinating history of the Qin dynasty, China's first imperial dynasty. We'll discover how **Emperor Qin Shi Huang created a unified Chinese empire** with these ten amazing facts!

31. **The Qin Dynasty was the first dynasty in the Chinese imperial era.** It lasted from 221 to 206 BCE.

32. **Emperor Qin Shi Huang conquered the six Zhou warring states,** unifying them into one country with a single government.

33. **He is also known for uniting the already-existing walls into the Great Wall of China** to protect his kingdom from invaders.

34. **During the Qin dynasty,** technology was significantly advanced. **Crossbows were used more often in warfare,** and **iron plows helped farmers grow crops** more effectively.

35. You might have heard of **the Terracotta Army. It was built to "guard" the tomb of Emperor Qin Shi Huang.** It consists of over eight thousand life-sized clay soldiers. These soldiers were all buried alongside the emperor in a secret underground complex near the city of Xi'an in central China.

36. At its peak, **the population of the Qin dynasty had tens of millions of people under its rule.**

37. **Emperor Qin Shi Huang created a standardized system for money** and weights and measures, which unified China's economy.

38. **A large number of books were burned and destroyed during his reign.** The emperor wanted to discourage people from learning about different ideas or teachings that he disapproved of, **such as Confucianism.** He even buried hundreds of Confucian scholars alive!

39. **The Chinese legal code was established during this period** and would be used for hundreds of years in the future; it focused mainly on values such as filial piety (respecting your parents).

40. **This dynasty lasted only fifteen years, but its cultural impact cannot be denied.** The Qin Empire standardized writing, expanded roads, and created a better postal system.

Han Dynasty
(202 BCE–220 CE)

Explore **the fascinating history of the Han dynasty**. Find out **how Confucianism became an official ideology during this period** and what impact it had on Chinese society. Also, explore the cultural exchange that took place due to **the Silk Road**. You might be surprised to learn what was traded!

41. **The Han dynasty was the second imperial dynasty of China** and lasted from 202 BCE to 220 CE.

42. **Liu Bang, better known as Emperor Gaozu, founded the dynasty** after he defeated his rival, **Xiang Yu**, the leader of **the rebel forces that overthrew the Qin dynasty**, in 202 BCE.

43. **Chinese culture flourished with advances in literature, art, music, and technology**. For example, in 132 CE, the Chinese invented an early form of a **seismograph for detecting earthquakes.**

44. **Confucianism**, which helped shape government policies and social values throughout East Asia, **became the official state ideology.**

45. **Chang'an** (modern-day Xi'an) **was the capital of the Han dynasty** for about the first two hundred years.

46. **Trade between China and other countries increased significantly during this period** due to improved transportation networks like canals or roads.

47. **The Silk Road trade routes were officially established, connecting China with central Asia, India, the Middle East, and Europe**. These routes were used for centuries by merchants traveling between countries with goods like silk, spices, and tea.

48. **The Han dynasty was divided into two periods: Western Han** (202 BCE–9 CE) and **Eastern Han** (25–220 CE).

49. **Emperor Wu of the Western Han is considered one of China's greatest rulers**. He expanded the borders to include parts of central Asia, Korea, and Vietnam.

50. **A civil service exam system was established** to allow people from all social classes to become government officials based on their knowledge instead of their birthright or wealth.

51. **The monetary system, which had been profoundly developed during the Qin dynasty, was further advanced**. New coins were added to make transactions easier.

52. **The first Chinese compass is thought to have been invented during the Han dynasty.** Originally called the **"south-pointing fish,"** it was not used for navigation but rather for fortune-telling and choosing building sites.

53. **Buddhism first arrived in China during the Eastern Han** period when **it spread from India through the Silk Road.** Traders brought scriptures back home with them after visiting foreign lands like Tibet or Nepal. Ideas and cultural aspects were traded just as much as goods!

54. **Emperor Wu sent a diplomat by the name of Zhang Qian to explore central Asia** and establish better trade routes in the 2nd century. He would quickly emerge as one of the most famous travelers.

55. **Zhang Qian also brought back knowledge that helped improve agriculture in China,** such as new crops like grapes and pomegranates.

56. **The Chinese social classes went through an interesting transformation during the Han period,** with the farmers rising in importance while merchants were considered to have been a lower class.

57. **Thanks to the opening of many new trade routes, advancements were made in Chinese medicine**, with doctors using acupuncture for injuries and the treatment of illnesses more akin to how we would today.

58. **The Great Wall of China was extended farther westward** during this era to protect against nomadic invasions from central Asian tribes like **the Xiongnu or Huns**, who threatened China's borders.

59. **The most recognizable parts of the Great Wall were built during the Han dynasty.**

60. **The Han dynasty used the decimal system** for counting and measuring.

61. **The Han also discovered square roots and cube roots!**

62. From 9 to 23 CE, **the Han dynasty was overthrown by the Xin dynasty**. After the Han dynasty was restored in 25 CE, Han rule was referred to as the Eastern Han.

63. Chinese literature flourished, with authors like **historian Sima Qian and historian/poet Ban Gu**. Their works are still being read and studied by people today.

64. **Zhang Heng, a famous Chinese astronomer**, noted around 2,500 stars and more than one hundred constellations!

65. **Artisans created beautiful pieces of pottery decorated** with intricate designs using glazes made from minerals found in nearby mountainsides or rivers.

66. Despite merchants' relatively low social status, **the merchant class managed to grow its wealth thanks to a lot of new trading routes.**

67. **Papermaking was invented during this time**. It was likely made using mulberry bark fibers, hemp, and rags. The invention of paper revolutionized communication.

68. **The Han dynasty is credited with inventing fireworks**, though its design differed greatly from later iterations of fireworks with gunpowder. People simply heated up bamboo sticks until they would sizzle and cause the air inside them to explode. For this reason, they were **called *baozhu* or "exploding bamboo."**

69. **Emperor Wu established an imperial university where students could study Confucianism**, literature, and other topics to become educated officials for government positions.

70. **The Han Dynasty started to decline after the death of Emperor Ling in 189 AD**. The instability created after the death of the emperor eventually caused the collapse of the dynasty after about thirty years of internal fighting.

Period of the Three Kingdoms
(220–280 CE)

Discover how different kingdoms fought for control over China, and learn about some of the legendary figures from this time, like **Cao Cao, Liu Bei, and Sun Quan.** Our twenty interesting facts will show you why this period is still remembered today!

71. **The Three Kingdoms was a time of chaos and war in ancient China,** lasting from 220 to 280 CE.

72. **The collapse of the Eastern Han dynasty led to the period of the Three Kingdoms,** with warlords fighting over control of China.

73. Three different kingdoms formed during this period: **Cao Wei, Shu Han, and Eastern Wu.** These kingdoms helped establish some semblance of peace.

74. Many **great generals** fought with each other for control over ancient China. **Cao Cao, Liu Bei, and Sun Quan** are just some examples.

75. **Cao Cao was a prominent statesman and warlord during the final years of the Han dynasty.** As one of the most influential figures of **the Three Kingdoms period**, he used his influence to create his own separate state named **Cao Wei** (or just Wei), though he never actually declared himself emperor.

76. **Liu Bei, another general of the Eastern Han dynasty, created his own state of Shu Han,** which was southwest of Cao Cao's Wei.

77. Another legendary figure from **the Three Kingdoms period was Zhuge Liang,** an incredibly wise strategist and advisor to **Liu Bei's army**.

78. Younger than his rivals Cao Cao and Liu Bei, the third most important warlord and ruler of the third of **the Three Kingdoms was Sun Quan**. He ruled the southern and eastern parts of China, which were organized into **the Kingdom of Wu.**

79. Eventually, prominent **general and politician Sima Yi gained power and orchestrated a coup d'état in Cao Wei,** emerging as the de facto ruler of the state from 249 to 251 before founding his own dynasty.

80. Many **famous warriors** became known for their skill and bravery, such as **Guan Yu and Zhang Fei!**

81. **The Three Kingdoms was a bloody period**, but Cao Cao and his sons were actually renowned poets!

82. In 260 CE, **the kingdom of Shu Han was defeated by the kingdom of Cao Wei**. Cao Wei would rule until **the Jin dynasty** took over in 266 CE.

83. Many great battles took place during this period. **The Battle of Red Cliffs**, which took place about twelve years before the start of **the Three Kingdoms** period, saw **Liu Bei and Sun Quan defeat Cao Cao's much larger army with clever tactics**. This battle helped decide the borders of two of the three kingdoms.

84. **The Three Kingdoms contested each other for power**, and their rulers all claimed the Mandate of Heaven—**the divine right to rule—at the same time**. While they were culturally and socially almost identical, there was no one "true" political entity of China during this time.

85. In 263, **the Kingdom of Shu Han fell. In 266, Sima Yan forced the ruler of the Kingdom of Wei to abdicate**. He created a new dynasty called Jin and became Emperor Wu of Jin.

86. **In 280, the Jin conquered Eastern Wu, unifying all of China under one banner.**

87. In the late 3rd century, about a decade after all of China had been unified, a series of internal conflicts, known as **the War of the Eight Princes**, helped bring about **the Jin dynasty's decline.**

88. **The Jin dynasty did not retain control for long**, lasting for less than 150 years. The dynasty fell to **the Song dynasty** in 420.

89. **Since the Three Kingdoms was a very exciting period**, the era is still remembered today through many TV shows, movies, books, and computer games.

90. **One of the most famous Chinese novels, *Romance of the Three Kingdoms*, is based on events that happened during this period.

Sixteen Kingdoms
(304–439 CE)

Explore **the fascinating history of China** during the period of **the Sixteen Kingdoms**. Discover why warlords fought each other while also unifying cultures. **Learn about powerful kingdoms,** and uncover how this period of fighting ended with these thirty interesting facts!

91. **The Sixteen Kingdoms was a chaotic time in Chinese history** that lasted from 304 to 439 CE.

92. The Sixteen Kingdoms period is interesting for historians because **it is one of the first large-scale conflicts in Chinese history** that was motivated by ethnic divisions to a large extent.

93. It began after the collapse of **the Western Jin dynasty** and ended with **the reunification of Northern China** in 439 by the Northern Wei.

94. **When the Western Jin dynasty collapsed, the Eastern Jin dynasty was established**. It ruled over southern China.

95. Despite its power, **it eventually collapsed due to a series of internal conflicts between rival factions** within the royal court and external invasions.

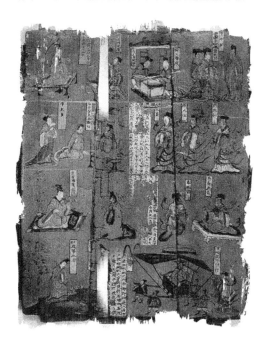

96. **In 291, a series of wars known as the War of the Eight Princes began**. Different princes and kings sought power over the Western Jin dynasty, which significantly weakened the dynasty and allowed other kingdoms to become more powerful at its expense.

97. **The Western Jin dynasty is important** for many reasons. For instance, it began to see **the Sinicization of non-Chinese people** who settled in the lands. This wasn't a state-run program, although that would happen later in **Chinese history**.

98. During the Sixteen Kingdoms period, **China was divided into several kingdoms ruled by different warlords**. These men constantly fought each other for control over territory and resources.

99. Although it is called **the Sixteen Kingdoms**, more than sixteen kingdoms emerged. Some kingdoms were just stronger than others.

100. Some historians believe **there were at least twenty-two "independent" political entities in China during this period**, ranging from smaller provinces to full-scale empires.

101. **States rose and fell**, which means these kingdoms were not fighting each other all at the same time.

102. Even though **each kingdom was politically independent**, the basis of their culture and traditions was mostly the same, though unique circumstances would sometimes lead to the development of different practices.

103. **The political instability led to massive population movements within China**, as people sought refuge from the conflicts between warring states.

104. **Sima Yan, the founder of the Jin dynasty**, was notorious for giving his family members a lot of power, something that ultimately contributed to the breakout of **the War of the Eight Princes.**

105. **There were many great military strategists during** this era. **Shi Le,** who once was a slave, rose up to become the leader of his own dynasty, **the Later Zhou**. Although **he is seen as a brilliant military mind,** he was unnecessarily cruel in his campaigns.

106. **Confucianism remained a staple philosophy during this era.**

107. **Buddhism also spread during this period**. Many monasteries were built in various cities across China.

108. **Yao Xing, ruler of the Later Qin dynasty, was a devoted Buddhist.** During his reign, Buddhism received official state support for the first time in China.

109. **The first Buddhist grottoes** (or caves) were carved during this period. It is believed **there were over one thousand caves in the Mogao cave system**. Today, there are over seven hundred Mogao caves. The ones built during the Sixteen Kingdoms have largely been lost.

110. Despite its political instability, **the Sixteen Kingdoms was a significant era for Chinese culture,** as it brought together different cultures and allowed people to exchange ideas.

111. **Cui Hong, a 6th-century historian, was the first person to use the term "Sixteen Kingdoms" in his writings.**

112. A contributing **factor to the collapse of the Western Jin dynasty was the immigration of the "Five Barbarian" clans,** who arrived in northern China during the late Eastern Han dynasty. Eventually, they played a role in overthrowing the Jin and organized their own states.

113. Coming mostly from modern-day Mongolia and central Asia, **the Five Barbarian tribes were not ethnically Chinese and lived nomadic lifestyles.**

114. **These non-Chinese peoples would eventually partially adopt Chinese customs and traditions,** especially when it came to administration and governance.

115. Literature from this period includes the works of **Tao Yuanming, a renowned poet also known as Tao Qian.** He wrote about everyday life in his native Fujian Province.

116. Among the newly established kingdoms, the only one that was able to unify a significant chunk of land for a longer time was **the Northern Wei, founded by the Tuoba people in 386 CE.**

117. Interestingly, because many of **the newly arrived foreign clans embraced Buddhism,** it spread as a prominent religion throughout northern China during this period.

118. **The Northern Wei chose Luoyang as its capital.** Having served as an ancient imperial capital, this choice was conscious, demonstrating the will of **the Tuoba to legitimize themselves and assimilate with the Chinese culture and people.**

119. **Culturally, this period of turmoil was not entirely stagnant as one might expect.** The discovery of terracotta statues dated to the Sixteen Kingdoms proves this.

120. **One famous battle during this time was the Battle of Fei River,** where two armies clashed on opposite sides of a river near modern-day Hefei.

The Period of the Northern and Southern Dynasties
[420–589 CE]

Explore **the rich history of the Northern and Southern dynasties** with us! This chapter will cover twenty astonishing facts about this era. Although **it was another chaotic time in history,** it also saw the rise of the arts. **Discover how religion, trade, and warfare shaped the culture of this era** and how great generals and poets left their mark on Chinese history.

121. **The Northern and Southern dynasties** saw the north and south of China separated into two separate kingdoms.

122. **Northern China was home to the Northern Wei**, which later split into the Eastern and Western Wei. **Northern Qi and Northern Zhou** would come at the tail end of this period.

123. **Southern China saw the rise of Liu Song**, Southern Qi, Liang, and Chen. These kingdoms did not coexist with each other.

124. **Despite being rivals from the beginning, neither one of the Northern and Southern dynasties managed to emerge as the most powerful entity in China.**

125. **During this period, Buddhism grew in popularity. Daoism** (or Taoism) was also embraced by the people.

126. **Many Buddhist temples were built during this era.** Some of these temples still exist, such as **the Shaolin Temple in** Henan Province or **the Yungang Grottoes** near Datong in Shanxi Province.

127. **Buddhist monasteries existed in parts of northern China.** There, monks would teach others about their religion while also **providing medical care**, education, and other forms of humanitarian aid.

128. **A big focus during this period was on paintings and sculptures**, which sometimes featured Buddhas.

129. **Poets wrote beautiful works about nature** inspired by the beauty they saw while traveling around rural areas throughout China. **Yu Xin and Wei Shou** are some notable examples.

130. **Emperor Wu of Liang**, ruling in the first half of the 6ᵗʰ century, was a notable patron of the arts.

131. **Many forms of arts were pursued**, most notably music and calligraphy, the latter of which had emerged as a very respectable art form.

132. **Prominent families dominated the power struggles in the Southern dynasties,** thanks in part to the powers attributed to the family clansmen by Cao Cao in the past.

133. **The Silk Road was still an essential part of the economy,** as it allowed merchants to transport goods from China to Europe with relative ease. This resulted in cultural exchanges between different countries, which helped spread knowledge about foreign lands.

134. **Advances were made in mathematics**, like calculating pi with more accuracy or developing new methods for solving algebraic equations.

135. **The Northern and Southern dynasties saw the introduction of new taxation,** coinage, and currency systems.

136. **The period witnessed a significant rise in trade with other countries**, which helped strengthen the Chinese economy through increased wealth and imported resources from abroad.

137. Much like during earlier periods, **the main power lay in the hands of generals and warlords,** who used the loyalty of their troops to rise to power and establish their own dominions.

138. During this period, **the non-Han (ethnically Chinese)** peoples who had migrated to northern China and had later risen to power, like **the Xianbei** and **the Tuoba**, became more and more assimilated with the Chinese culture to be more fit to rule their Chinese subjects.

139. **Landscape paintings became very popular in China** due to their vivid colors and excellent brushstrokes, capturing the beauty of nature with great detail.

140. **The Northern and Southern dynasties ended after Emperor Wen of the Sui dynasty declared himself ruler of all of China,** unifying both northern and southern parts under his reign in 589.

Sui Dynasty
(581–618 CE)

This chapter will **explore the fascinating Sui dynasty**, which lasted from 581 to 618 CE. Examine an array of interesting facts about the period and its key figures, including **Emperor Wen and his son Yang Guang**. We will also look at aspects of **Chinese culture** and how they impacted the next dynasty, the famous Tang dynasty.

141. **The Sui dynasty was a Chinese imperial dynasty** that lasted a short time, from 581 to 618 CE.

142. **Yang Jian, who took the name Emperor Wen,** founded the dynasty and later became its first emperor.

143. During this period, **essential infrastructure projects were built, such as canals, roads, and bridges,** to help expand transportation and trade in China.

144. **To build these projects, the Sui government conscripted workers.** This move led to tensions, as the people had to deal with conscription and heavy taxation.

145. **Emperor Wen improved education during his reign** by introducing a national civil service examination system, which helped people get jobs in the government based on their abilities rather than family connections or wealth.

146. **One of the most notable achievements from this era was the Grand Canal.** It linked the northern and southern parts of China, helping to unify the country.

147. **Sections of the Great Wall were repaired during the Sui dynasty** to provide more safety to the northern part of China.

148. **The Sui dynasty promoted Buddhism throughout its reign**, with Chinese schools of Buddhist thought becoming more prominent. It is thought that the flourishment of Buddhism allowed the Chinese culture to reemerge stronger than ever.

149. **Emperor Wen was succeeded by his son Yang Guang (Emperor Yang),** who began to rule in 604 CE. **Emperor Yang was known for his extravagance** and lavish lifestyle, which significantly weakened the dynasty's finances.

150. **Japan was a strong trade partner of the Sui dynasty**, while Korea and Vietnam were among the two chief external enemies of China at the time.

151. In 617 CE, **General Li Yuan led a successful coup against Emperor Yang due to anger over high taxes**, which eventually resulted in the overthrow of the Sui dynasty in favor of **the Tang dynasty**, beginning a new era of prosperity under their rule.

152. During this period, **Chinese culture flourished with painting, music, and literature**.

153. Interestingly, **the last Sui emperor and Emperor Wen's successor, Yang Guang, was also one of the most renowned poets of this period**.

154. **Emperor Wen, who devoted a lot of funds to the military**, managed to assemble a force that was several hundred thousand men strong and marched them to **battle against the Chen on the Yangtze River**.

155. **The Sui military campaigns against Vietnam were partially successful**. Northern Vietnam was retaken (it had been under the control of the Chinese during the Han and Jin dynasties), but further pushes into the south were abandoned due to difficulties that the Chinese armies encountered.

156. Despite **the Sui dynasty's** relatively short rule, it made many lasting contributions that shaped China, such as **the Kaihuang Code**. This law code got rid of harsher punishments and replaced them with punishments that were more accepted by the people. These punishments are harsh by today's standards, but being banished or beaten with a big stick sounds a lot better than being torn limb from limb!

157. **The Tang dynasty didn't change much of what the Sui dynasty had established**. For instance, the Tang rulers based their laws **on the Kaihuang Code**.

158. **The ambitious and lavish endeavors of the Sui emperors eventually greatly depleted the dynasty's finances,** contributing to its relatively quick decline.

159. **The war with the Korean Kingdom of Goguryeo was deadly**. None of the four expeditions the Sui launched ended in success.

160. **The fall of the Sui dynasty marked the end of a brief** but influential period that helped shape China's future, especially in regard to culture and religion.

Tang Dynasty
(618–907 CE)

The Tang dynasty is considered one of the more well-known dynasties of China. It saw the flourishing of culture and advancements in technology. You might be shocked to learn what was discovered during this time, and you might be even more shocked to learn that **we use many of those inventions still!**

161. **The Tang dynasty started in 618 and ended in 907 CE**. There was a brief break in the empire, lasting from 690 to 705.

162. **During the Tang dynasty, Chinese culture flourished** with advancements like printing, a form of paper money, and the creation of gunpowder.

163. **The capital city during this period was Chang'an** (now known as Xi'an).

164. **One of the greatest rulers of the dynasty was Emperor Taizong.** His reforms and achievements increased China's prosperity and stability during his reign, which lasted from 626 to 649.

165. **The Tang dynasty is known as the Buddhist golden age.** Although **most of the emperors were Daoists,** they greatly supported Buddhism, with the government having control over monasteries.

166. **Women had more rights than before**. They could engage in political discussions and were no longer required to wear long dresses or cover their faces.

167. **The relative period of stability under the Tang made the Silk Road trade routes much more active**, with more reliable routes being established and maintained.

168. **The most famous poet of the Tang dynasty was Li Bai**, who wrote about patriotism and nature in a spiritual manner.

169. **The Tang Dynasty reached its golden age under Emperor Xuanzong** (685-762), which was marked by economic and political stability and prosperity.

170. **Emperor Xuanzong was also admired for his patronage of the arts and education,** which attracted a lot of poets, philosophers, and artists to his court.

171. Unlike in the past, **the Great Wall of China was not extended** to any great length during the Tang dynasty

172. **Buddhism started to be used for political purposes by rulers like Empress Wu Zetian,** who declared herself an enlightened ruler supported by Buddhist doctrine.

173. To assert her dominance, **Wu Zetian introduced new characters for a brief period of time into the written language,** though the changes were reversed after her death.

174. **The Tang dynasty saw a precursor to Chinese opera called *canjunxi* become popular.** *Canjunxi* originated from folk music, and *canjunxi* later told concise stories.

175. **The invention of gunpowder is attributed to Chinese monks and alchemists during this period.** Gunpowder is believed to have been invented around 850. It eventually spread to Europe via contacts with merchants on the Silk Road.

176. **Tea became popular among all classes** due to its medicinal properties and was exported abroad as far away as Japan.

177. **The Tang dynasty is known for its ceramics**, many of which have been found in archaeological sites around the world.

Martial arts, such as Shaolin kung fu, took off during this time. Martial arts were practiced for health benefits and self-defensive purposes.

178. **The population increased significantly throughout the dynasty** from an estimated fifty million people at its start to perhaps around seventy-five million by 900 CE.

179. **The use of umbrellas became more common during the Tang dynasty.** People used them to protect their clothing from rain, but umbrellas were also used to provide shade from the sun.

180. **Painting flourished with notable artists, such as Wu Daozi and Zhang Xuan,** painting on silk, wooden boards, walls, and ceilings.

181. **The recently established Imperial Examination System was expanded and used more commonly during the Tang times,** contributing to the creation of a new class of ruling elites. Still, as the system was still relatively new, it took the Chinese civil servants a bit of time to adapt to it.

182. **Pancakes became quite popular during the Tang dynasty.** Eating beef, on the other hand, was discouraged.

183. **The first recorded Christian missionary arrived in China in 635.**

184. **Eunuchs became notable figures in court due to their closeness to the emperor,** with some achieving significant influence over policy-making decisions.

185. **Stability and the flourishing of the Silk Road trade routes** allowed new goods, practices, and fashions to enter China for the first time after a long era of turmoil

186. **Domestic trade routes also developed,** thanks to the repairs done to the Grand Canal.

187. **The Tang dynasty was a period of great cultural exchange,** with many foreign diplomats, traders, and missionaries from as far away as Japan, India, and Persia bringing their ideas and beliefs to China.

188. **Establishing diplomatic relations with other nations like Korea led to increased trade between them,** such as the export of silk cloths or lacquerware.

189. Although **the Tang dynasty launched military campaigns,** they were not as successful as previous dynasties.

The Five Dynasties and Ten Kingdoms Period
(907–960 CE)

Let's go from **the golden age of the Tang dynasty** to another chaotic time in Chinese history. Discover fifteen fascinating facts about **the Five Dynasties and Ten Kingdoms period!**

190. **The Five Dynasties and Ten Kingdoms period** was a time of political fragmentation in China, lasting from 907 to 960 CE.

191. **During this period, five dynasties ruled over northern China** one after the other, and more than **twelve independent kingdoms** (together known as the Ten Kingdoms) ruled the south, often at the same time.

192. **All of these political entities based their political structures on the preceding Tang dynasty.**

193. Although this was a chaotic time, **Buddhism was still promoted**, especially in the south.

194. **One might assume that the economy declined since China was facing internal wars, but it actually saw economic growth!**

195. **The Five Dynasties of the North were Later Liang, Later Tang, Later Xin, Later Han, and Later Zhou.**

196. **They all succeeded each other** from 907 to 960, occupying the same territory and plagued with instability and warfare.

197. **The Five Dynasties and Ten Kingdoms period** ended in 960 when the Song dynasty unified China under one rule.

198. **The Ten Kingdoms,** on the other hand, were located in the southern part of China. They included **Yang Wu (907–937), Wuyue (907–978), Min (909–945), Ma Chu (907–951), Southern Han (917–971), Former Shu (907–925), Later Shu (934–965), Jingnan (924–963), Southern Tang (937–976),** and **Northern Han (951–979).**

199. Unlike **the Five Dynasties** of the north, some of **the Ten Kingdoms** existed together for brief periods of time, overlapping with each other.

200. Due to this, it is considered that **southern China was much more stable** than the north during this period.

201. Prominent artists from this period include **Li Cheng and Xu Xi**, whose artistic styles place a big emphasis on the depiction of nature as a sacred entity.

202. **This period of divide in the north ended with the Song dynasty's** reunification of northern China in 960.

203. **Serious political divides between the north and the south were expressed in the development of strong regional identities,** some of which would last for long periods of time.

204. **The period of the Five Dynasties and Ten Kingdoms** is another example of an era of strong political divide in China, exemplifying the cyclical nature of Chinese history.

Liao Dynasty
(907–1125 CE)

The Liao dynasty existed alongside the Five Dynasties and Ten Kingdoms, as well as the Song dynasty, earning it a spot in the history books. This section **will explore the history and culture of this intriguing empire** through twenty amazing facts.

206. **The Liao dynasty was founded by the Khitan people** in 907 and lasted until 1125.

207. At its height, **the dynasty ruled northern China, Mongolia,** northern **Korea,** and parts of **Russia.**

208. **The Khitan people came from the steppes of Mongolia.** They expanded in the 9th century and eventually declared themselves to be a dynastic state of China.

209. **The Khitans had been known to the Chinese for centuries.** Their earliest mention in Chinese sources appears in **the *Book of Wei*,** which was completed in the 6th century.

210. **Buddhism was the most popular religion,** although the Liao religion blended Buddhism with the tribal religion, **Confucianism,** and **Daoism.**

211. **The Liao had a strong military with cavalry units that protected their borders** from invaders, like **the Song dynasty** to the south or nomadic tribes from central Asia.

212. **Their economy relied heavily on trade along the Silk Road** routes, which connected them with other cultures across Eurasia.

213. **They developed a writing system known as Khitan small script,** which allowed them to keep records of taxes or laws passed by rulers.

214. If there is a small script, there has to be a large script. Both **Khitan scripts were based on the Chinese script.**

215. **The Liao emperors could read Chinese**, which likely proved helpful to them. **Some Chinese works were translated into Khitan**, but it is not known for sure what. It is likely that **the Confucian classics were never translated**.

216. **Khitan women enjoyed greater freedoms**. For instance, women were taught how to hunt and could even manage property when their husbands were away.

217. **Liao dynasty art was varied**, but the dynasty is best remembered for its **sculptures**.

218. **No one knows for sure where the term Liao comes from**. Some believe it might come from the **Khitan word for iron**.

219. **The Liao dynasty might have used gunpowder weapons in battles.**

220. The later **Liao empire is remembered for its religious tolerance** and openness to different cultures.

221. **Administration in the lands controlled by the Liao dynasty was split into two**. One part was focused on **the Khitan population**, which was mostly concentrated in the northern part of the empire, while the southern one focused on **the Han Chinese population**.

222. **The army of the Liao was divided into different sections**. The most elite corps was comprised **of Khitan heavy cavalry**, while **the ethnic Chinese usually were the militia.**

223. **The Liao dynasty did not have a significant naval presence.** Instead, it depended on land armies to fend off enemies.

224. **In 1125, the Liao dynasty was conquered by the Jurchens,** who founded **the Jin dynasty** in its place.

225. **After the dynasty fell in 1125, some of its territories were absorbed by the Song or Jin dynasty,** while others became independent states ruled by nomadic tribes from central Asia, such as **Qara Khitai.**

Song Dynasty
(960–1279 CE)

This chapter will explore **the incredible history of the Song dynasty, one of the most prosperous periods in Chinese history**. Examine its advances in technology and art to see how its culture is still influential today.

226. **The Song dynasty lasted from 960 to 1279 and is divided into two periods: Northern Song and Southern Song**. The Southern Song dynasty was founded in 1127 and lasted until 1279.

227. **Zhao Kuangyin** (later known as **Emperor Taizu**) **founded the Song dynasty** after staging a coup to end **the Later Zhou dynasty**, which was the last of **the Five Dynasties**.

228. **China had one of its most prosperous periods during the Song dynasty** with advances in science and technology. **The population increased dramatically**, and the arts flourished.

229. **The first recorded chemical formula of gunpowder dates to this period**, which led to new weapons like cannons and firearms being used for warfare.

230. **Kaifeng was the Northern Song's capital city** during this period. It was located on the Yellow River. **The Southern Song's capital was Lin'an** (today's Hangzhou).

231. **The Song dynasty was the first Chinese dynasty to establish a permanent standing navy**, which allowed it to emerge as a powerful maritime power.

232. **Neo-Confucianism emerged as an influential philosophy**, emphasizing personal morality over politics or religion. **Neo-Confucianists wanted to bring back the Confucianism of old**, as the philosophy had mixed with other religions over the centuries.

233. **True north was discovered for the first time by using a compass.**

234. Important advancements were made in sanitation and urban hygiene. For example, **the Song dynasty built free public toilets in big cities.**

235. **These public toilets actually sold fecal matter to farmers**. Farms used the poop as fertilizer!

236. **Women were still seen as being lower than men on the social ladder**, but they were given more rights than before. Under special circumstances, a woman could own some of her father's property if he died.

237. **Foot binding became popular among upper-class women** who wanted smaller feet since they were seen as more graceful.

238. **The Song dynasty was the first to invent a movable printing press.** The moving pieces were made of porcelain.

239. **New star catalogs were created by astronomers like Su Song.** He also invented a water-powered armillary sphere, which tracked celestial movements accurately over time.

240. **The Song dynasty introduced the mariner's compass,** which allowed sailors to navigate more accurately.

241. During this period, Chinese literature flourished with famous poets like **Su Shi, who wrote about his travels in China, and Li Qingzhao, who wrote romantic poems** about love and nature.

242. **Art during this time included landscapes and portrait paintings. Calligraphy was another major art** form during the Song dynasty.

243. **This dynasty saw a growth in trade with other countries** like Japan and Korea through its port city Quanzhou (then known as Zaiton).

244. **Chinese porcelain became popular globally** due to its high quality and intricate designs.

245. **Tea drinking was popular during this time**, as it was a way to socialize with friends or family members over tea ceremonies.

246. **This dynasty saw increased literacy rates among men and women** due to improved education systems throughout China.

247. **Hangzhou's West Lake was a most famous tourist attraction during this era**, and it still exists today! It has been praised by many poets throughout history for its beauty and tranquility.

248. **Xiangqi, which is a Chinese version of chess, and the board game Go became popular.** These games were played recreationally and competitively.

249. After a series of political rivalries weakened the Northern Song by the 11th century, **the Northern Song was overthrown by the Jurchens, who would establish the Jin dynasty** in 1127.

250. **The Mongol Empire eventually conquered the Southern Song dynasty** in 1279, ending its rule over China. However, many of its inventions, ideas, and culture remain influential to this day.

Jin Dynasty
(1115–1234 CE)

The Jin dynasty took over the Northern Song dynasty in 1115 and lasted 119 years, ending in 1234. **Learn about how culture developed in the Jin dynasty** and how the dynasty finally fell apart with these twenty facts.

251. **The Jin dynasty was founded by the Jurchen people** in 1115 CE.

252. **The Jurchen were tribes that lived in northeastern China.** They were unified under Wanyan Aguda, who became **Emperor Taizu of Jin.**

253. **Emperor Taizu of Jin unified northern China after defeating rival warlords** and establishing a strong central government.

254. **He moved his capital from Huining to Yanjing** (modern-day Beijing) in 1153. He also created a southern capital, Bianjing (modern-day Kaifeng).

255. **After their conquest, about three million Jurchens migrated to China.** Although **they were the minority**, they ruled the ethnic Chinese population of the empire, which almost outnumbered the Jurchens ten to one.

256. **After having defeated the Northern Song, the Jin dynasty chose earth as its dynastic element.** According **to the Five Elements practice of the Chinese culture**, earth comes after fire—an element that was associated with the Song—making this choice deliberate and symbolic.

257. **The Jin dynasty is credited with creating a unified currency system** by introducing paper money in 1160, replacing coins.

258. **The Jin dynasty developed differently than the Southern Song dynasty.** This was mainly because the two empires did not communicate with each other and were rivals.

259. **The Jin were known for being the first to use gunpowder effectively in warfare,** although they did not win the battle.

260. **The Jin Dynasty added to the Great Wall of China, although they built their parts of the wall differently.** They would dig a ditch and then build a wall inside of it.

261. **Under the Jin, Daoism underwent great transformations**, growing as a religion, with the dominant **Quanzhen School being founded** in the 1160s.

262. **Emperor Shizong** (r. 1161–1189) **promoted Jurchen traditions**. He declared that government officials should speak in Jurchen instead of Chinese.

263. **The emperors of the Jin dynasty had two names**. The first one was their Jurchen name, while they also adopted Chinese names and were given posthumous titles.

264. **The mighty army of the Jin dynasty was heavily comprised of mounted warriors**, something that had to do with the origins of the Jurchens.

265. **Despite its strength on land, the Jin dynasty suffered catastrophic losses at sea**, with the navy being defeated multiple times by the Song armies.

266. **The government of the Jin**, much like preceding non-Chinese rulers, **tried to adopt Chinese customs and forms of governance** while trying to combine them with Jurchen traditions.

267. Due to internal political squabbles, **the Jin dynasty declined drastically after having suffered military defeats at the hands of the Song** in the late 12ᵗʰ century.

268. In the 13ᵗʰ century, **Emperor Xuanzong decided to attack the Southern Song to assert his dominance but was defeated**, much like his ancestors about half a century before. This further contributed to the Jin dynasty's decline.

269. In 1211 CE, **Genghis Khan invaded northern China and captured Yanjing** in 1215, forcing **the Jin court into exile in Manchuria**.

270. **The Southern Song dynasty helped the Mongols take down the Jin dynasty**, which came to an end in 1234.

Yuan Dynasty
(1271–1368 CE)

The Yuan dynasty is notable for many reasons, one of which is Marco Polo's visits to China. Explore how **Mongol rule** differed from dynasties that came before, and find out why the dynasty came to its inevitable end.

271. **The Yuan dynasty was the first foreign dynasty to rule over all of China.**
272. **Kublai Khan, leader of the Mongol Empire and grandson of Genghis Khan, founded the dynasty.**
273. Chinese culture flourished in many areas. **The Four Masters of Yuan were renowned for their artwork,** with later artists trying to emulate their style.
274. **Marco Polo visited during this period** and dictated his travels to a fellow prisoner. **Rustichello da Pisa wrote the famous book** *The Travels of Marco Polo*, which helped spread knowledge about China throughout Europe.

275. Although **the stories in *The Travels of Marco Polo* are interesting**, they are also fantastical. Some historians believe that Marco Polo might have never stepped foot in China at all.
276. **The capital of the Yuan dynasty was Dadu** (modern-day Beijing). This was the first time Beijing was the capital of all of China.
277. **The Mongols tried to bring paper money to places outside of China**, but it was viewed as foreign, so the people didn't trust it.

278. **The Yuan dynasty supported Buddhism and Confucianism,** although many religions, including **Christianity and Islam, were practiced.**
279. **Since the Yuan dynasty was tolerant of most religions,** the number of Muslims in China rose significantly.
280. **Gunpowder weapons were used extensively by armies.** The Mongols relied on bombs and cannons to fight their enemies.

281. **Kublai Khan promoted growth on the Silk Road and provided loans to finance trade caravans**, which allowed the economy to prosper.

282. **Carrots, turnips, and cotton were some of the things that became popular during this dynasty.**

283. **The Great Wall of China was repaired and extended by Mongolian soldiers.**

284. **Tea drinking became popular** among people living in China, with tea houses established in cities like Beijing and Hangzhou.

285. **Most works were still printed with block printing**, but some were printed with moveable type. **The Mongols printed many books**, giving us many sources to examine today.

286. **The Yuan dynasty was the first to use the abacus for calculations in China.**

287. **The Mongolian language never fully supplanted Chinese.** In fact, most of the inscriptions from this period are written in both languages.

288. **The Yuan dynasty introduced a new writing system called the 'Phagspa script.** This writing system was meant to be a unified script for the lands the Mongols conquered.

289. **Despite the strength of the Mongol army at the time, Kublai Khan was unable to conquer Japan.** His invasions in 1274 and 1281 all failed. The Japanese were able to partially stop the Mongols, but heavy storms and unfavorable conditions at sea created further problems and also contributed to their defeat.

290. **Internal problems and natural disasters led to the Yuan dynasty's decline.** When the Red Turban Rebellion broke out, the Yuan rulers were not strong enough to fight back.

Ming Dynasty
(1368–1644 CE)

It is time to explore another iconic era in Chinese history: the Ming dynasty. We will discover information about **Zheng He, religion, and weaponry**. The Ming dynasty is well known for its cultural contributions; let's find out why!

291. **The Ming dynasty was the fourth-longest dynasty in Chinese history,** stretching from 1368 to 1644 CE.

292. **Peasant rebel leader Zhu Yuanzhang founded the dynasty.** He later declared himself **the Hongwu Emperor** and established **the capital in Nanjing** in 1368.

293. **The early years of the Ming dynasty were marked by reforms,** including land distribution, tax reduction, and suppression of powerful families.

294. **Great achievements made during the Ming included advances in shipbuilding and navigation technology which allowed for explorations.** One of the most notable was Zheng He's voyages to Southeast Asia, the Middle East, and Africa between 1405 and 1433.

295. **The Chinese population increased dramatically under the rule of this dynasty.** It is hard to know the exact numbers since the population figures from this period are not exact, but some historians believe that around **two hundred million people called China home.**

296. **The modern bristle toothbrush was invented in China in 1498.**

297. **The famous Forbidden City in Beijing was built during the Ming dynasty.** The Forbidden City saw twenty-four emperors sit on its throne over a span of five hundred years.

298. **Chinese artisans were known for using vivid colors** and intricate designs, like the blue and white porcelains that this era is well known for.

299. **Buddhism, Daoism, and Confucianism were the three most important religions/philosophies during this time.** Chinese folk religions were also practiced by the people.

300. **The *Yongle Dadian*, an encyclopedia, contained thousands of volumes from all areas of study.** Most of the volumes have been lost, but it was considered the world's largest encyclopedia until Wikipedia knocked it down a peg.

301. **Gunpowder weapons were used extensively and developed by leaps and bounds.** By the end of the Ming dynasty, European-style firearms were popular.

302. Many great works of literature emerged. **Authors like Feng Menglong wrote stories about ordinary people.** Social issues played a prominent role in poems and stories during this dynasty.

303. **The Grand Canal was extended and linked with natural waterways**, allowing a sea trade route from Beijing to Hangzhou.

304. **Neo-Confucianism became very popular during the Ming dynasty**, although it later faced scrutiny. Some scholars, like **Wang Yangming, believed that people who had not experienced the real world were not as wise as those who had**, stating that peasants with real experience were wiser than officials.

305. This dynasty also saw some famous works of literature, such as *Journey to the West* **and possibly** *Water Margin*.

306. **Traditional forms of theater were admired by all classes**, with puppet operas being a particularly favored form of entertainment.

307. **The Ming dynasty enacted sumptuary laws, which tried to relegate how much people bought.** For instance, merchants and commoners could not wear silk.

308. **At the beginning of the Ming dynasty, the power of the eunuchs was restricted.** As time passed, more control was given to them. They built their own social structures and sometimes rivaled the emperor in power.

309. **China became increasingly isolated during the Ming dynasty, closing its borders to foreigners.**

310. **Ming rule ended in 1644 when rebel forces led by Li Zicheng overthrew the last emperor Chongzhen in Beijing.** He declared a new dynasty, which took control of the country until 1911.

Qing Dynasty
(1644–1911 CE)

Explore the fascinating history of the Qing dynasty. Learn about several famous rulers of this period, and discover the advancements that were made. The last imperial dynasty of China has much in store, so let's dive in!

311. **The Qing dynasty was the last imperial dynasty of China** and lasted from 1644 to 1911.

312. **The Manchu people, originally from northeast Asia and descended from the Jurchens, ruled the dynasty.**

313. **The Shunzhi Emperor was the second emperor of the Qing dynasty but the first to rule over all of China.** He took the throne he was only five years old!

314. **The Kangxi Emperor is considered one of the most exceptional Chinese emperors** and reigned for sixty-one years—longer than any other Chinese ruler in history!

315. During **the Kangxi Emperor's reign,** customs houses **traded with foreign countries. Open trade with the West** wouldn't happen until after **the Opium War** of 1842.

316. **The Eight Banners were military divisions, with soldiers being organized into units based on their ethnicity and social status.** The Qing dynasty relied on them for military campaigns, but over time, the Eight Banners stopped being an effective fighting force.

317. **Emperor Qianlong had an exceedingly successful reign.** Historians believe the Qing dynasty was at the height of its power during his rule.

318. He commissioned **the largest collection of Chinese books** that we know of, **the *Siku Quanshu* or the *Complete Repository of the Four Branches of Literature.*** It included almost thirty-seven thousand volumes!

319. **During this period, China's contact with the outside world increased dramatically**. European powers, such as **Russia and Great Britain**, colonized parts of China and bordering regions, leading to territorial disputes that would last for centuries.

320. **The opium trade between British India and Qing-ruled provinces created immense profits** for merchants and caused chaos in many parts of the country due to drug addiction.

321. **Emperor Tongzhi attempted to modernize China during his reign with Western technologies**, such as railroads, telegraph systems, hospitals, and schools. He died before he could finish it.

322. **Empress Dowager Cixi was the one who came up with the idea of modernizing China,** as the country needed a boost to survive.

323. **Although Empress Dowager Cixi never officially ruled in name**, she was a regent and ensured her nephew sat on the throne after her son died so she could maintain power.

324. **Empress Dowager Cixi did not approve of Western governance,** but she did think that some Western reforms would help strengthen the country. By the end of her life, she began to embrace the idea of a constitutional monarchy.

325. **Han Chinese men were required to wear their hair in a pigtail called a queue,** which was how the Manchu men wore their hair. The Han Chinese hated this law, as it reminded them that they were no longer in control of China.

326. **The Kangxi Emperor tried to put a stop to foot binding,** but he was unsuccessful. Foot binding would only be banned in 1912.

327. **The Qing dynasty saw an increase in literacy rates due to widespread education** initiatives, which, in turn, led to great works of literature being devoured by the populace.

328. One famous piece of literature was *Dream of the Red Chamber*. This book has been studied extensively and even has its own field of study called **Redology!**

329. **Confucianism was promoted by many emperors,** but its emphasis on social harmony and obedience to authority hindered technological progress and progressive policies, things that were taking place elsewhere in the world.

330. **The Chinese inoculated against smallpox and saw a decrease** in the infant mortality rate because of advances in medicine.

331. **Women began to write more during this period**. They mostly wrote poetry.

332. At the height **of the Qing rule, China was so powerful** that it forced many of its neighboring states to pay tribute.

333. **Tea was China's biggest export**. In the early 19th century, tea accounted for 90 percent of exports out of Canton.

334. **The Yongzheng Emperor banned Christianity**. He also started programs to help combat famine and poverty in rural regions.

335. **Calligraphy and painting remained popular pursuits**. The Four Wangs were prominent painters from this period.

336. **Railroads were introduced to China** for the first time during the Qing dynasty.

337. **The series of reforms** that attempted to pursue modernization in the late 19th century would be referred to as **the "Self-Strengthening Movement."** The reforms impacted some of the most important aspects of life, such as the economy, military, and education.

338. **Empress Dowager Longyu declared an end to imperial rule** on February 12th, 1911, on behalf of the six-year-old emperor, Puyi.

339. In 1917, **Zhang Xun tried to restore the Qing dynasty**, but he failed.

340. **Puyi would later become the puppet emperor of the Japanese-**controlled state of Manchukuo, which fell at the end of World War II.

The Opium Wars
(1839–1842, 1856–1860 CE)

The Opium Wars were fought between China and various Western powers, namely Britain. Why did they start? What did they accomplish? We will take a look at these questions and uncover some other interesting facts along the way.

341. **The First Opium War was a war between China and Britain**, which lasted from 1839 to 1842.

342. **It started because the Chinese government wanted to end the opium trade**. Opium is a drug made from poppy plants. The British did not want to end such a lucrative trade.

343. **During the war, several battles were fought**. The Chinese war junks, a type of ship with sails, were often overpowered by the British navy, which possessed larger ships with cannons mounted on them.

344. **After almost three years of fighting, Britain won the war** due to its superior weapons and military technology compared to China's forces.

345. **China had to give up Hong Kong Island to Britain**. It also **had to open ports in Guangdong Province** so British merchants could legally sell opium there without restrictions.

346. **This significant event caused tensions between Chinese citizens and foreign governments.** These tensions are still felt to this day.

347. **The Treaty of Nanking, which ended the First Opium War**, was the first of what are called unequal treaties. These treaties gave more power and control to Western powers while granting China very little in return.

348. Opium is highly addictive. The Treaty of Nanking did not include any provisions to address the problem. It is believed the number of opium addicts nearly doubled after the treaty was signed.

349. The Second Opium War started because of a dispute over trading rights, and it involved not only Britain but also France and other Western powers.

350. In October 1860, **the Summer Palace was looted by British and French soldiers**. Priceless works of art were taken to Europe.

351. **The Second Opium War ended with the signing of the Treaty of Tientsin** (1858) and the Convention of Peking (1860). These treaties further expanded trade privileges for Western powers, legalized the opium trade, and led to more territorial concessions for China.

352. **The Opium Wars contributed greatly to the decline of China as a regional and world power**, turning it into almost a semi-colonized state.

353. **By 1870, China's global GDP had fallen by half**. Historians believe the drop was a direct consequence of the Opium Wars.

354. **The Opium Wars were the first precedent of the unfair relationship** that would eventually develop between the industrialized West and 19th-century China, which was trailing behind in technological and social advancements.

355. Despite the West's victory, **many critiqued the Opium Wars for their imperialist nature and the domination of the Chinese by the Europeans**. Criticisms came from intellectuals, such as Karl Marx, who condemned the West's actions in the war.

Taiping Rebellion
(1850–1864 CE)

This section will explore the fascinating **Taiping Rebellion**, one of the most important events in **the Qing dynasty**. We'll look at ten interesting facts about its leader and his followers' beliefs. We'll also discover **the changes that this rebellion brought** about.

356. **The Taiping Rebellion was a civil war in China** that lasted from 1850 to 1864.
357. **It was fought between the Qing dynasty**, which ruled China, and a rebel group called **the Taiping Heavenly Kingdom**.
358. **Hong Xiuquan, the commander of the rebellion**, believed God had chosen him to lead his people out of suffering and poverty. He actually said that he was the brother of Jesus Christ.

359. Though the exact number of casualties is disputed, **it is believed that at least twenty million people died during the Taiping Rebellion,** making it one of the bloodiest events in recent Chinese history.
360. **The Taiping Rebellion is the bloodiest civil war in history**. Both sides engaged in massacres against the other, although most deaths happened because of disease and famine.

361. **The success of the rebels varied from year to year**, but the Qing government was eventually able to suppress the rebellion. This was partially due to the rebels' lack of organization, as well as reluctance from foreign powers to aid them.
362. During its peak, **the Taiping Heavenly Kingdom controlled over half of modern-day China,** including major cities like Nanjing (once known as Nanking).

363. **Women played an essential role in this rebellion**. They served as soldiers, nurses, and even generals in **the Taiping army**. It was rare for women to serve in a fighting capacity at this point in the 19th century, making the Taiping army unique.

364. **Although this rebellion was one of the factors responsible for imperial China's decline,** it also gave the Chinese emperors a chance to strengthen China so it could stand strong on the world stage.

365. **The rebellion led to important short-term changes in Chinese society**, such **as Han officials gaining more power in government.** Provincial armies became more important, replacing the imperial forces. These would play a factor in the eventual end of the Qing dynasty.

Tongzhi Restoration
(1860–1874 CE)

Let's uncover **ten amazing facts about the Tongzhi Restoration**. Improvements were made to many areas of Chinese society and government, **which helped to strengthen China** and bring it more into the modern era.

366. **The Tongzhi Restoration was a period in China that lasted from 1860 to 1874.**

367. During this time, **the Chinese government worked to restore order and stability** after years of civil wars and foreign invasions.

368. The name of this period was derived from the title of **the Tongzhi Emperor,** who ruled from 1861 to 1875.

369. Although the period was named after **the Tongzhi Emperor, it was his mother, Empress Dowager Cixi, who came up with the ideas of how to make China strong** once more.

370. **Many reforms were made during this era,** including improvements to education, transportation systems, military organization, and taxation policies. **These reforms helped strengthen the Chinese economy and society.**

371. **The Tongzhi Restoration opened a foreign office to deal with diplomats,** which helped open China up more to other countries.

372. **Although the Tongzhi Restoration did modernize some things,** Empress Dowager Cixi clung to the old traditions. Historians believe this caused the period not to reach its full potential.

373. **For the most part, the reforms did not reach their full potential** because the government was unsure how to implement them.

374. **China reformed its military during this time,** but it was unable to score a decisive victory in **the Sino-Japanese War**.

375. **The Tongzhi Restoration did help strengthen traditional Chinese values,** which brought some unity to the country.

The First Sino-Japanese War
(1894–1895)

Japan and China both sought to be the major power in the East. The tensions between the two finally exploded with **the First Sino-Japanese War**. Let's look at ten facts about this war and how it impacted China.

376. **The First Sino-Japanese War was fought between July 1894 and April 1895 over Korea.**

377. **Korea had long been under China's sphere of influence**. In 1876, Korea was opened up to trade with Japan.

378. **Japan worried that Korea was too underdeveloped.** The Japanese government believed that if Korea was unable to defend itself, Western powers would swoop in and take it over.

379. **When China sent forces to help put down the Tonghak Rebellion in Korea**, Japan claimed it violated a previous treaty, which eventually led to a declaration of war.

380. **China also had to deal with a rebellion in northern China while fighting the First Sino-Japanese War**. Chinese Muslims rebelled against the Qing government because it refused to declare which Sufi order was superior.

381. **The Qing dynasty was forced to sue for peace after six months of warfare.**

382. **China was no longer the dominant power in East Asia**, as Japan had emerged as the clear winner of the war.

383. **China lost around thirty-five thousand men** (dead and wounded), while Japan suffered around five thousand casualties.

384. **The Treaty of Shimonoseki saw China recognize Korea's independence** and ceded the Liaodong Peninsula, Taiwan, and the Penghu Islands to Japan.

385. **Japan would go on to invade Taiwan in 1895 since a number of officials refused to recognize the treaty and instead set up a democratic republic**. Japan was eventually able to annex the island.

Boxer Rebellion
(1899–1901 CE)

Discover **the story of the Boxer Rebellion**, a two-year conflict in China between foreign powers and Chinese rebels. This chapter **will explore ten interesting facts about this rebellion**, from its origins to its eventual defeat.

386. **The Boxer Rebellion was a rebellion in China against foreign influence and control.**

387. **It started when Chinese people formed the Society of Righteous and Harmonious Fists,** an organization to fight against foreigners taking over their country.

388. Since many of **the rebels practiced martial arts, the English called them "Boxers."** The name must have stuck!

389. During the rebellion, **the Boxers attacked foreign embassies, churches, and businesses across China** but primarily in Beijing (the capital of China).

390. **To put down the rebellion, eight countries sent troops to help defeat the rebels.** These countries were **Japan, Russia, Britain, Germany, Austria-Hungary, Italy, the US, and France.**

391. **After two years of fighting, the international forces defeated the Boxers in 1901,** but it took another decade to fully restore peace between China and the other nations and to address the domestic issues caused by the rebellion.

392. **Any government official who supported the Boxers was executed,** and China was forced to pay a huge indemnity to the eight-nation alliance.

393. **Empress Dowager Cixi, who was still the main power behind the throne, supported the Boxers.** Later, she made nice with the Western powers, agreeing to make changes that would **turn the country into a constitutional monarchy.**

394. **The Qing dynasty tried to repair the damage created by the Boxers,** but the dynasty was weakened. The reforms that it tried to enact were not enough, leading to **the end of the monarchy in 1911.**

395. **Although Western powers played a big role in the Boxer Rebellion, Japan emerged as the dominant power.** In time, Japan would control a good chunk of East Asia, including parts of China.

The 1911 Revolution
(1911–1912 CE)

The 1911 Revolution was a pivotal moment in human history. The Qing dynasty was overthrown, ending the imperial rule of China. Discover what took the monarchy's place and other interesting trivia about this revolution with these fifteen enthralling facts.

396. **Another name for the 1911 Revolution is the Xinhai Revolution.** It is named after the year it took place on **the Chinese calendar**.

397. **Although the 1911 Revolution was successful**, it was far from the first uprising to rock China in the late 19th and early 20th centuries.

398. **Sun Yat-sen, the leader of the 1911 Revolution**, participated in many of the earlier uprisings.

399. **In 1894, Sun Yat-sen formed the Revive China Society** (Xingzhonghui). A year later, another prominent rebel group, **the Furen Literary Society**, merged with the Revive China Society.

400. **Sun Yat-sen was in exile during this time**; he created his revolutionary party in Honolulu, Hawaii.

401. **In 1905, the Revive China Society would transform into the Kuomintang or KMT.** This is still a major political party in China today.

402. Although uprisings had occurred in previous years, **the Wuchang Uprising in October 1911 is considered the event that kicked off the 1911 Revolution.** Other regions soon followed, with people fighting against the Qin dynasty.

403. In 1911, **Yuan Shikai, a military official, was appointed prime minister by the Qing dynasty** to deal with the rebels.

404. **The Republic of China was created in January 1912. Sun Yat-sen would become its first president.**

405. **Sun Yat-sen would be president for a little over two months**. Yuan Shikai would become president in March.

406. **To become president, Yuan Shikai had to get Emperor Puyi to abdicate**. Since the emperor was so young (he was only six), his regent, **Empress Dowager Longyu, had to sign the papers for him.**

407. **Life did not change much for the average Chinese**. The biggest thing that changed was the abolishment of feudalism.

408. **There was a lot of anti-Manchu sentiment after the revolution. In Beijing,** thousands of Manchu people died in violent attacks.

409. **Four thousand years of imperial rule ended when the Qing dynasty was overthrown.**

410. **As time passed, the Chinese became divided again**, with some seeing the 1911 Revolution as the final stage for a democratic China and others seeing it as a stepping stone for a greater revolution.

Yuan Shikai's Attempt to Reestablish Imperial Rule
(1915–1916)

Although **Yuan Shikai became president of China**, he wasn't content with the level of power he was given. **He wanted to return back to the monarchy**. Let's look at five interesting facts about his reign, including how **he declared himself emperor** and why his attempt failed.

411. **Yuan Shikai quickly secured power as president**, which allowed him to gather support when he wanted to return to **the traditional way of ruling**. In December 1915, he was elected emperor.

412. **Yuan Shikai became known as the Hongxian Emperor**.

413. **The revolutionaries did not like this move, and neither did Yuan Shikai's military officials.** The people rebelled, and when **Yuan Shikai did not perform well in the battles**, he lost foreign support.

414. **Yuan Shikai only ruled for eighty-three days.**

415. **When he died in June 1916, his death left a power vacuum**, with many warlords racing to fill it themselves.

Warlord Era
(1916–1928 CE)

Discover **the turbulent history of China during the Warlord Era**. This chapter will explore five interesting facts about this period, including how it finally ended.

416. **The Warlord Era was a time of chaos and conflict in China**, as many different warlords fought for control of the country.

417. **The main fight was between the Kuomintang government's army and Yuan Shikai's former government's army**, although other groups rose up as well.

418. The biggest battle of this period was **the Central Plains War**. Over one million soldiers fought in it!

419. **The Warlord Era ended with the Northern Expedition**, led by **Chiang Kai-shek**, in 1928, which united most of China under one rule again.

420. **Warlords continued to pop up and create serious threats for the next few decades**, which added to China's instability.

Chinese Civil War
(1927–1949 CE)

This chapter will explore **the tumultuous history of the Chinese Civil War**. Explore ten interesting facts about this conflict, including how it was fought and who ultimately won.

421. **The Chinese Civil War was a conflict between the Communist Party of China and the Nationalist** (Kuomintang) Party of China.

422. **It lasted from 1927 to 1949**, although there was a break in the fighting when **the Chinese put aside their differences to fight Japan** and aid the Allies in World War II.

423. There are no exact records of how many died, but **millions of people were killed or displaced due to fighting** and famine.

424. **The Communist Party of China was supported by the Soviet Union**, while **the Nationalist Party of China received support from the United States** and other Western countries.

425. **As the years passed, the communist forces gained more followers**. By 1945, they had over three million troops at their command.

426. **The Chinese Civil War resumed in 1946 when Chiang Kai-shek led an assault on northern China.**

427. Both sides committed war crimes. **The Nationalist forces conducted the White Terror, killing hundreds of thousands of people who were suspected of being communists.** The communist forces targeted landlords, as they wanted to redistribute the land to the peasants.

428. In October 1949, **Mao Zedong's communist forces won control over most of mainland China and established the People's Republic of China** (PRC).

429. **Chiang Kai-shek and around two million Nationalist soldiers retreated to Taiwan**, where their government, **the Republic of China** (ROC), was formed.

430. **The Republic of China laid claim to China proper until 1988. The People's Republic of China claims sovereignty of Taiwan**, even though it has never controlled any part of it.

The Second Sino-Japanese War
(1937–1945)

The Second Sino-Japanese War was a devastating conflict that is often overshadowed by World War II. This section takes a look at how the war began and some of the atrocities that were committed.

431. **The Second Sino-Japanese War took place from 1937 to 1945.** The war is sometimes **called the Asian Holocaust.**

432. **Japan invaded Manchuria in 1931 and eventually established a puppet state called Manchukuo,** which was headed by **Emperor Puyi, the last Qing emperor.**

433. **In July 1937, a Japanese force demanded entry into Wanping, near Beijing,** to look for a missing soldier. The Chinese stationed there refused. Shots were eventually fired. Many see this as the beginning of **the Second Sino-Japanese War.**

434. **During the Second Sino-Japanese War, around twenty million people were killed.** Most of them were civilians.

435. **This war is notable for the Nanjing massacre, also known as the Rape of Nanjing.** The massacre lasted around six weeks and saw anywhere between 40,000 and 300,000 civilians die.

436. **Looting, rape, arson, and murder took place during those six weeks.** Some in Japan downplay the incident, with some even claiming the event never took place. **Japan has yet to apologize for the massacre,** which is a source of tension to this day.

437. **By 1939, the Japanese controlled most of China's larger cities,** but they could not advance much in the countryside, where members of **the Chinese Communist Party used guerilla tactics to keep the Japanese at bay.**

438. **When Japan attacked Pearl Harbor in 1941, the US increased its aid to China.** The US gave China around twenty billion dollars in today's money, giving the Chinese a fighting chance against the Japanese forces.

439. **In 1945, Japan surrendered because of the atomic bombings of Hiroshima and Nagasaki.** China regained its lost territories **and became a permanent member of the UN Security Council.**

440. **Once World War II ended, the Chinese Civil War continued,** with the Communists eventually winning.

People's Republic of China
(1949–Present)

The People's Republic of China is often in the news today, but how much do you know about it? These fifteen interesting facts will give you a better idea of the PRC in general; the next few sections will take a look at its history.

441. **The People's Republic of China was founded in 194**9 and is **the second-most populous country in the world after India**, with over 1.4 billion people living there.

442. **Today, China has twenty-three provinces, five autonomous regions, four direct-controlled municipalities, and two Special Administrative Regions** (SARs). The two SARs are Hong Kong and Macau.

443. **Beijing is China's capital city**. It is China's **second-largest city** in terms of population, with **Shanghai being the first**.

444. **Mandarin Chinese is the official language used in both China and Taiwan**, although other dialects are spoken.

445. Although **China is an atheist state**, it **recognizes four religions: Daoism, Buddhism, Islam, and Christianity.**

446. **Confucianism isn't regarded as a religion by most**, although its teachings are still celebrated today.

447. **China has many UNESCO World Heritage Sites** that preserve its rich cultural past.

448. **Peking duck, dumplings, and noodles are all popular dishes in traditional Chinese restaurants.**

449. **China has more billionaires than any other country besides the United States.**

450. **Chinese have to attend school for at least nine years**. Many go on to attend university.

451. **As of 2023, China is the most popular country in Asia** for international students looking to receive a higher education degree.

452. **In 2013, China became the world's largest trading nation**. Most of what China trades is electronics and clothing.

453. **Giant pandas have become an unofficial symbol of China because China would gift pandas as a way to establish diplomatic relations**. Giant pandas are native to China. The pandas you see in zoos are on loan from China, so they technically belong to the Chinese government.

454. **Chinese currency is called renminbi or people's currency**. Most nations outside of China call it **the yuan**, which is the basic unit of **the renminbi**.

455. **China has become one of the largest economies in recent years** due to its booming manufacturing industry.

Cultural Revolution
(1966–1976)

The Cultural Revolution of China sought to preserve communism in China. However, it **has been criticized for causing the nation distress**. Let's look at ten facts about this period to see what happened.

456. **The Cultural Revolution in China was a time of notable change** and upheaval, lasting from 1966 to 1976. **Mao Zedong was the leader of China** during this time.

457. **The Red Guards, which were student military organizations, were encouraged to destroy historical artifacts** and architecture so the people wouldn't be reminded of the past.

458. **People had their personal belongings searched by Red Guards** when they were accused of being traitors or enemies of communism. There could be deadly consequences for those found guilty.

459. **Artistic expression was heavily censored during this period**. Books, films, music, and theater performances that did not promote communist ideals were banned or drastically altered before being released into public circulation.

460. **Millions of Chinese citizens left for other countries** due to political turmoil caused by the revolution's harsh policies.

461. **Many massacres took place. The Guangxi massacre saw tens of thousands of people die in cruel ways.** Cannibalism was even encouraged by local communist officials. There was no famine; people were motivated to do this for political reasons.

462. **People belonging to the Five Black Categories were considered enemies of the state.** These categories were landlords, counter-revolutionaries, rich farmers, "bad elements," and people belonging to conservative parties.

463. **Even senior government officials were accused of betraying China.** Liu Shaoqi, who had served as chairman of the PRC from 1959 to 1968, was accused of supporting capitalism. He died in prison.

464. **Intellectuals were persecuted, and universities were shut down**. Opportunities for rural-educated children rose, while those in the cities, especially those belonging to wealthier families, saw fewer opportunities to advance.

465. **The Cultural Revolution continued after Mao's death, ending with the arrest of the Gang of Four**, a group that held significant sway during **the Cultural Revolution**.

Reform and Opening-up
(1978–Present)

This chapter will explore **the remarkable transformation of Chinese society** since 1978. Discover fifteen amazing facts about how this period impacted China's economy and society.

466. In 1978, **the Reform and Opening-up period took place** when China started opening its economy to other countries.

467. **This period allowed people to buy more things**, start businesses, and travel abroad for the first time in many years!

468. **There has been a consistent decline in the number of Chinese people living in poverty** since 1978.

469. **Foreign investment has grown significantly over the past few decades**, helping create jobs in China's cities and rural areas.

470. **Farmers were allowed to sell their produce directly to markets** instead of going through government-run stores, which helped increase incomes drastically.

471. **There have also been notable improvements** in healthcare coverage and educational opportunities in China since the reforms began.

472. **In 1979, Deng Xiaoping introduced the one country, two systems approach**, which allowed **Hong Kong and Macau to have a different economic and political system** than China proper.

473. In 1984, **fourteen Special Economic Zones were set up** in coastal cities to encourage foreign investment. These areas have rapidly developed into some of the most prosperous regions in China today.

474. **Reforms also included creating more effective legal systems**, increasing religious freedom, and allowing people more personal freedoms, such as choice over marriage partners and careers.

475. As part of its reform efforts, **China has signed bilateral agreements like trade deals with other countries**, becoming an increasingly active member of the international community.

476. **China is one of the largest economies globally by GDP**. Some analysts believe **it will take over the US** in about a decade.

477. **The Chinese government has invested heavily in research and development**, coming up with many new inventions **in technology and medicine.**

478. **China is the world's largest exporter**, with exports of over $2 trillion in 2018. This was only made possible with the reforms that started in 1978.

479. In recent years, **China has become a key player in digital technology, including artificial intelligence and blockchain,** which are considered essential tools for future economic development.

480. **The Reform and Opening-up period changed Chinese society dramatically** by creating new opportunities while improving living standards across the country.

Tiananmen Square Protests
(1989 CE)

The Tiananmen Square protests of 1989 have gone down in history as one of the most iconic moments for democratic movements. These five facts will provide some basic information about what happened.

481. **On June 4th, 1989, a peaceful protest happened in Tiananmen Square in China** to call for more freedom and democracy.

482. **The Chinese government sent troops to break up the protest**. They did so violently, with thousands dead and wounded.

483. **History may never know how many people actually died**, as the Chinese government refuses to release the official figures. **The official number is three hundred deaths**, but eyewitness accounts place the number much higher.

484. **The protests were largely influenced by Hu Yaobang's death**. He was a pro-reform politician who was forced to resign, dying shortly after his resignation because of a heart attack.

485. **One of the most iconic images of the 20th century took place during the protests when the picture of one man standing in front of a line of tanks was captured**. It is unknown what happened to this man.

Rise of China
(1990s–Present)

This chapter will explore the remarkable history and development of China from 1990 to the present day. These fifteen facts will provide some hard data as to how far China has come.

486. By today's standards, **China is one of the most modern countries in the world**. According to the 2017 statistics, all of its population has access to electricity.

487. From 1979 to 2017, **China's economy grew at an average rate of 10 percent**, making it one of the fastest-growing economies in history.

488. Since 1990, **notable advancements in healthcare have happened**. Infant mortality rates decreased, and life expectancy increased.

489. Since 1979, **over seven hundred million Chinese have escaped poverty due to economic growth** and reforms implemented by the government.

490. **China joined the World Trade Organization** (WTO) in 2001, which opened up its markets for international trade, leading to increased foreign investment and growth opportunities for businesses within its borders.

491. **China's space program achieved a milestone by launching the first Chinese into orbit aboard a Shenzhou-5 in 2003.** The country continues to make strides in space exploration.

492. **China is a permanent member of the UN's Security Council**. This once again proves the country's international importance.

493. **The Belt and Road Initiative** (BRI) **launched by President Xi Jinping** in 2013 aims to bring together more than 150 countries by cooperating on large-scale infrastructure projects. **China is looking to take on more of a leadership role** with this initiative.

494. **Although China has made much progress, there is still much work to be done**. In recent years, **China has been accused of human rights violations**, particularly **against the Uyghurs**.

495. **In addition, one of the biggest problems modern China is facing has to do with pollution**. Compared to other big countries, it still lacks green infrastructure and is the world's largest polluter of air.

496. In 2021, **China invested a record-breaking $378 billion in research and development projects**, advancing its technology and innovation capacity.

497. **High-speed railways are crisscrossing long distances at record speeds**, while motorways connect different cities like never before.

498. **Chinese citizens have greater access to technology** due to rapid developments in 5G network capabilities and internet infrastructure.

499. **As wealth has spread across China, cities have seen notable growth**, with towering skyscrapers appearing in Shanghai and Beijing.

500. Over the past thirty years, **the Chinese government has made great strides toward improving their standard of living** and creating jobs and new opportunities for future generations.

Conclusion

Our journey through Chinese history has been long but fascinating. We have **seen great dynasties rise and fall,** periods of **turmoil and revolution,** and times of peace and prosperity. We have witnessed warlords, civil unrest, and **massive social reforms.**

China's remarkable rise on the world stage is likely to continue, and the nation will undoubtedly continue to be in the news in the decades to come. **China has made great strides toward improving the people's lives,** although there is still much criticism by other countries over how the government operates.

This book has offered readers a look at some key facts that shaped Chinese history. Hopefully, some of these facts were new to you. And hopefully this book has piqued your interest into **reading more about China's fascinating past.**

Part 2: Japanese History
500 Interesting Facts About Japan

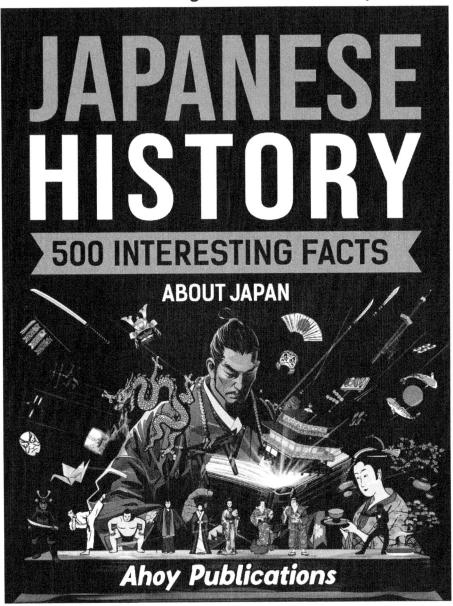

Introduction

The history of Japan is filled with fascinating cultural, economic, and political developments. This book dives deep into each period of **Japanese history**, from the nation's earliest beginnings in prehistoric times up to the present day, and examines the events and forces that have propelled it forward.

Beginning with a look at **prehistoric Japan**, you will get a taste of what life was like in ancient times. Explore eras like **the Yayoi period, the Kofun period, and the Asuka period.**

This book also looks at important events in **Japanese history,** such as **the Meiji Restoration, the Japanese Constitution of 1947,** **Japan's economic miracle** in the 1950s, and so much more.

Examine crucial issues like **the 1973 oil crisis, the bubble during the 1980s,** and **the "Lost Decade."** The book concludes with an overview of contemporary cultural changes after 2000 and political developments and international relations up until today.

Take a journey through time as we **explore over two thousand years of Japanese history.**

Prehistoric Japan

This chapter will delve into the captivating history of prehistoric Japan. We'll explore twenty **captivating facts about the beliefs, tools, and art** forms that were developed during this period. Learn why **bronze weapons** played an important role in warfare and how **pottery techniques** advanced. All of these aspects made a profound impact on Japanese society at the time.

1. **Prehistoric Japan lasted from around 35,000 BCE to 500 CE.**
2. **The earliest period, the Paleolithic era, ended around 13,000 BCE,** giving rise to **the Jomon period. The Yayoi period** came after, starting around 300 BCE and ending around 250 CE. **The Kofun period** lasted from 250 until 538 CE.
3. **People in prehistoric Japan** lived by hunting animals, gathering plants, and fishing for food.
4. **They made their homes out of straw and wood** or dug caves into the earth called pit houses.
5. **The first pottery in Japan was decorated with rope-like patterns,** which gave it its name "Jomon," meaning "cord marks." The first pottery in Japan was made in the early Jomon period, around 10,500 BCE.

6. Around 1000 BCE, **bronze weapons were introduced to be used for hunting game** or fighting enemies.

7. **The Jomon culture was first discovered by archaeologists in the late 19th century.**
8. **The first major excavation of a Jomon** site was conducted in the early 20th century at **the Omori site in Tokyo.** This excavation revealed a large number of Jomon artifacts, including pottery, figurines, and stone tools.
9. **The Jomon people sometimes carved symbols during this time called Kamiyo moji** ("characters of the Age of Gods"). These were likely not letters. They might have been symbols of magic and protection.
10. **Rice farming began in the late Jomon period,** around 400 BCE.

11. From 300 BCE on, **iron tools and weapons were used in Japan.**

12. By 250 CE, **political leaders and extended families began to form organized clans or tribes** that competed with each other for power over the country's resources, like land and water.

13. Around 300 BCE (or perhaps even earlier), **bronze mirrors were introduced from China,** but they were not widely used until many centuries later. Mirrors would later play a role in Japanese mythology.

14. **Bronze mirrors slowly became an important symbol of status in Japanese culture.** They are still used today as part of some traditional ceremonies.

15. **During prehistoric Japan, the Japanese believed that all natural phenomena, animals, and plants possessed kami, or divine power.** Kami could also refer to a god or spirit and can be used to describe something sacred.

16. **Artwork, such as sculptures and masks made out of wood or clay,** became popular during this period. They were often decorated with paint or lacquer for an even more impressive effect, but the use of lacquer and paint was limited at this time.

17. **Music played an important role in prehistoric Japanese society.** Instruments like whistles and drums were likely used to entertain people at festivals and ceremonies celebrating religious events or special occasions like weddings.

18. **Clay figurines from the Kofun period have been found with holes in them,** which suggest they were used as flutes.

19. By 300 BCE, **pottery techniques advanced so much that vessels could be fired in kilns rather than just dried over fire pits.** This allowed the Japanese to make pots with different shapes, colors, and textures.

20. **During this period, trade was limited to the Japanese islands.** Trade between groups on the islands was relatively limited due to geography and the lack of effective transportation.

Yayoi Period
(300 BCE–300 CE)

Explore the ancient history of Japan during the Yayoi period in this chapter. We'll discover twenty interesting facts about **their culture, lifestyle, and language.** The Yayoi people are remarkable for many things, such as **irrigation systems, advances in fishing techniques, and alliances with other tribal groups.** We'll also uncover evidence of ancestor worship, shamanism, and more!

21. **The Yayoi period lasted from around 300 BCE to 300 CE.** It was the third major period of Japanese history.

22. **The Yayoi people are believed to have crossed from mainland Asia to Japan through Korea.**

23. **This period is named after a region in Japan** where early evidence of the culture appeared in archaeological sites in 1884.

24. **The early Yayoi people were farmers who used irrigation systems made with bamboo pipes,** which brought water from rivers or springs into the fields.

25. **They also hunted, gathered wild plants, and fished for food sources,** such as shellfish or small fish found in shallow waters near shorelines, during this period.

26. **Rice cultivation became an important part of the economy by 200 BCE** when it spread through mainland Asia along trade routes connecting eastern and western Asian cultures.

27. **Many historians credit the Yayoi people with developing wet-rice cultivation** (meaning rice fields constantly contain water). This technique generally produces a higher yield.

28. **During the Yayoi period, metal tools, including bronze and iron, were introduced and used to craft items like weapons, jewelry, and agricultural implements,** marking a significant technological advancement for the time.

29. **Dental care during the Yayoi period remains unclear,** but evidence suggests the use of resin-like materials on teeth, potentially offering some protection or pain relief.

30. In 250 CE, an **official imperial court and government began to form in Yamato** (now Nara Prefecture) with their own language called Yamato kotoba, which is still spoken today in the imperial court.

31. **The Yamato period, when the government ruled from Yamato,** overlaps other periods in Japanese history, mainly the Kofun period and the Asuka period.

32. **Artifacts from this time include haniwa figures, clay sculptures depicting people, animals, or shapes.** These were usually found around tombs or burial sites.

33. Over time, **tribes formed alliances to gain access to resources** like land or food during times of scarcity throughout the Yayoi period.

34. **The Yayoi people brought their own language and culture with them.** Over time, **the Yayoi people** mixed with the earlier **Jomon people,** who were hunter-gatherers. The descendants of these two groups are the modern Japanese people.

35. **Large family groups known as clans rose to prominence during the Yayoi period.**

36. **During this period, shamans** (religious leaders) had a significant role in society. They served both spiritual and therapeutic roles, like healing sicknesses or interpreting dreams.

37. **Shamans were responsible for mediating between the human and spiritual worlds,** and they were also involved in divination and other religious practices.

38. **Burial mounds from this era provide evidence that some kind of ancestor worship took place during this time.**

39. Around 300 CE, **trade routes opened up between China, Korea, and Japan,** allowing goods like ceramics, silk, and metals to be exchanged.

40. **During this period, there were advances in fishing techniques that allowed for larger catches and more food sources.** However, until the 19th century, Japanese vessels usually stuck to the coastal waters.

Kofun Period
(300– 538 CE)

This chapter will explore the interesting history of the Kofun period, which was a time of great change and development in Japan. It is named after **the large earthen mounds called kofun,** which were built to be tombs for important people. During this period, Japan became more unified, and **the Yamato clan emerged as the dominant power.**

Let's learn more about this important time in Japanese history!

41. The Kofun period of Japan started in 300 CE and lasted until 538 CE.

42. It is divided into two parts: **the Early** (300–400 CE) **and Late** (400–538 CE) periods.

43. **During the Kofun period, society was divided into clans,** with nobles at the top, followed by commoners. Commoners were the lowest social class. They were farmers, artisans, and merchants.

44. There are limited historical records, but there is evidence that Japan had slaves during this period.

45. **The imperial family** (the Yamato clan) assumed control over much of eastern Japan. Local clans held power in the western regions.

46. **Powerful nobles and warlords rose**, often forming alliances or marriages rather than fighting each other to gain more control.

47. **Japan began using Chinese characters around the 1st century CE,** but only for basic understanding. By the 5th century, they had adopted **the Chinese kanji writing system.**

48. **The Japanese later developed methods like kanbun to write Japanese using Chinese characters with pronunciation hints.** The first Japanese text, **the Kojiki,** used this method.

49. In terms of architecture during this era, **large burial mounds known as kofun were built to commemorate important people or events.** Palaces were also constructed for various powerful rulers all over Japan.

50. **New laws were introduced during the Kofun period,** but these were not codified laws; those came much later. These laws were more like local customs and codes of behavior.

51. **During the 5th century CE, there was considerable trade between Japan and China,** which brought foreign goods into the country. This trade included silk cloth or coins made from gold and silver.

52. **The Yamato clan believed they were descended from the gods,** a concept known as "Kami no Mago" (descendant of the gods), which served as a cornerstone of their legitimacy and power.

53. By 500 CE, **horseback riding and archery had become popular in Japan, as these skills were important for warriors.** Warriors were an integral part of society during this period. **The samurai,** as we know them as a class, did not develop until the later Heian period.

54. It is plausible that **the Japanese adopted the dao from China during the Kofun period,** which they later modified to create the katana.

55. **The katana is more curved than the dao, and it is also made from different types of steel.** The katana was likely created during the Heian period.

56. **Fishing became a lucrative industry by 500 CE,** so much so that it eventually led to the accumulation of wealth by those involved in the trade. This helped cause an increase in population.

57. **Poetry was popular among the upper classes during the Kofun period,** forming the early roots of Japanese poetic traditions.

58. By 500 CE, **the Japanese were building rudimentary shrines in populated parts of the country.** These shrines venerated the early gods, nature spirits, and dead leaders.

59. During this period, **battles between rival clans took place,** but they usually ended quickly due to the lack of resources or manpower.

60. **The Kofun period in Japan transitioned to the Asuka period** around 538 CE. The transition was marked by cultural shifts like Buddhism and political developments.

Asuka Period
(538–710 CE)

This chapter will explore **the fascinating history of the Asuka period in Japan.** We'll uncover twenty interesting facts about this period, including the introduction of **Buddhism and new technology.** Artwork flourished during this period, as did the government. Let's explore why this period was so important.

61. The Asuka period began in the year 538 and ended in 710.

62. **During this period, much of Japan was united,** at least in name, under one ruler for the first time.

63. One of the most influential men in Japanese history was **Prince Shotoku Taishi,** who governed as regent for a time in the late 6th and early 7th centuries.

64. **Prince Shotoku is credited with helping to unify Japan under one ruler,** promoting **Buddhism**, and **adopting Chinese culture** and learning.

65. **Buddhism was introduced to Japan during this period from Korea and China.** The religion brought many new cultural practices, such as art styles, literature, music, philosophy, and more. Buddhism helped shape Japanese culture.

66. **Prince Shotoku is credited with bringing about a centralized government** based on Chinese models of governance.

67. **The Japanese government was also based on Confucian principles** such as respect for authority figures and society at large. These ideas would become an integral part of Japanese culture known today as wa, or harmony between individuals within a larger group context.

68. In 604, **Prince Shotoku wrote the Seventeen-Article Constitution,** which outlined how people should live their lives **according to Buddhist teachings** and moral codes of conduct.

69. **Temples and shrines dedicated to Buddhism were built throughout the Asuka period,** many of which still stand today as important cultural landmarks in Japan.

70. **The Kojiki** (Record of Ancient Matters) was compiled during this period and is an **important text that chronicles the early history of Japan** from its founding up until 628 CE. It was completed by court scholar O no Yasumaro in 712.

71. **While compiled in the 8th century, the Nihon Shoki and Fudoki offer windows into the Asuka period** by weaving written records with oral traditions. Though valuable sources, these glimpses of the past require careful evaluation to differentiate historical reality from cultural reinterpretations.

72. **The Asuka period saw advances in technology, such as metallurgy, with iron weapons being manufactured for military use,** and papermaking becoming widespread across the country, leading to increased literacy rates among the upper classes.

73. **Commoners were not taught to read because it was not considered necessary for them.** They were expected to work in the fields or in other manual labor jobs.

74. **The Asuka period is named after the Asuka region of Nara Prefecture,** where the capital of Japan was located during this time. The Asuka region was a major center of political, economic, and cultural activity during this period.

75. **Artwork flourished, with sculptures depicting religious figures being carved out of wood or made from lacquer.** Mural paintings adorned temples throughout the country, adding color to these sacred spaces.

76. **Poetry was also popular during this time, such as tanka.** The tanka is a thirty-one-syllable poem and often focuses on emotions.

77. **Craftsmen were highly skilled in metalworking, creating intricate bronze mirrors often decorated with images related to Buddhism or scenes from nature.** These items would be used for both practical purposes and ritual offerings at shrines.

78. **The Asuka period saw the rise of powerful clans, such as the Soga clan,** which had a strong influence over politics during this time.

79. **Japan's first native-made coins were minted during this period.** People used currency for trade and commerce. Bartering was still popular, though.

80. **While no single event marks a hard stop, the move of the Japanese capital from Asuka to Nara** in 710 CE is widely considered the symbolic transition from the Asuka to the Nara period.

Nara Period
(710–784 CE)

This chapter will explore **the intriguing history of Japan during the Nara period.** We will learn many interesting facts and discover how **Chinese culture influenced art, architecture, and literature.** A lot of exciting developments happened during this period, so let's dive right in!

81. In 710 CE, **Emperor Gemmei moved the capital of Japan from Fujiwara to Heijo-kyo** (modern-day Nara). The name for this period, which lasted from 710 to 784 CE, comes from this change in capitals.

82. **Nara was a major center of culture and learning during its time as the capital.** Many important temples and shrines were built in Nara, including Todai-ji Temple, which is home to the Great Buddha of Nara.

83. **The Great Buddha of Nara, a bronze statue built in the 8th century,** stands fifty feet tall. Today, tourists from all over the world visit the statue.

84. **Buddhism started to become more popular during this period.** Many Buddhist texts were brought over from China.

85. **Chinese culture had a major influence on the Nara period. Its writing system, architecture, and even food** were adopted and then adapted to the growing Japanese culture.

86. **A unique system of land ownership called shoen was developed during this time,** which helped protect farmers from being exploited by powerful aristocrats. This was somewhat effective. Later, in the samurai period, farmers and other commoners had virtually no rights.

87. In 743 CE, **Emperor Shomu ordered temples to be built throughout Japan to spread Buddhism to all parts of the country.**

88. **The most famous artwork produced during this period is known as the Yakushi Triad,** which was moved to Nara when the capital moved. It consists of a sculpture depicting **the Healing Buddha** flanked by two bodhisattvas made out of bronze.

89. **Though the Nara emperors ruled a large part of Japan,** they did not have complete control over much of the country. The northern island of Hokkaido was not considered part of Japan proper until 1869.

90. **Hokkaido is a land of extreme climate, snow, and mountains.** It was inhabited by the aboriginal Ainu people, who were forcibly assimilated by the Japanese in the 19th and 20th centuries.

91. **Many great literary works were written during this time, such as the Man'yoshu,** which is a collection of more than 4,500 poems. **The Man'yoshu** is the oldest extant collection of **Japanese poetry.** It was compiled in **the Nara period by Otomo no Yakamochi** (718–785), a court poet and scholar.

92. **The Nara period marks the beginning of formal Japanese diplomatic relations with other countries.** Diplomatic missions and ambassadors from China and Korea started visiting Japan in 736 CE.

93. **Though it was known in other periods, the famous sake rice wine** began to be produced in mass quantities during **the Nara period.**

94. **Traditional festivals like the Gion Matsuri originated around the Nara period,** possibly to please the gods for good harvests. While early connections to the 7th century exist**, the Gion Matsuri's established annual celebration** likely solidified later, evolving into the renowned festival we know today.

95. **The Nara period played a nuanced role in the evolution of Shintoism.** Increased documentation with Buddhist influence helped standardize practices. Shinto deities blended with Buddhism. Buddhist features were added to shrines.

96. **Local shrines and common practices preserved Shintoism's core.** Records from the Nara period laid the foundation for later Shinto revivals and distinct philosophies.

97. **Shintoism is the indigenous religion of Japan. It is a polytheistic religion that believes in many gods called kami.** Kami can be anything that is considered sacred or powerful, such as mountains, rivers, trees, and even animals.

98. **Shintoism does not have a founder or a sacred text. It is based on oral traditions and practices that have been passed down for generations.**

99. **Shintoism is a way of life that emphasizes the importance of nature, purity,** and ritual. Shintoism does not proselytize, and it does not require its followers to believe in anything in particular. It is a personal religion that each individual can interpret in their own way.

100. For centuries, **in Nara, Sika deer** (often called "Nara deer") roam freely. They are revered **as messengers of Shinto gods.** Protected as national treasures, they symbolize the region's cultural identity and attract tourism.

Heian Period
(794–1185 CE)

This chapter will explore **the engaging history of the Heian period.** We'll take a look at twenty **interesting facts about Japan's culture during this time.** Art flourished, with important achievements in **painting, calligraphy, and poetry.** Powerful warriors emerged too, and this period is known for its architectural accomplishments.

101. **The Heian period began in 794 CE when the capital of Japan was moved to modern-day Kyoto.** It ended in 1184.

102. **The term "Heian" means "peace" or "tranquility,"** which is a reflection of the period's political stability and economic growth.

103. **Kyoto became the center of Japanese politics during this period. Emperor Kanmu built a palace** and large gardens for his court in Kyoto.

104. **Art flourished during the Heian period, with advancements in painting, calligraphy, poetry, music, and literature.** The Heian period is often referred to as Japan's golden age.

105. **Hand-copied books became popular during this period,** with upper-class people copying Chinese texts for entertainment or educational purposes.

106. **Copying Chinese texts contributed to the development of calligraphy skills** and a deeper understanding of classical **Chinese language and culture** among the educated elite in Japan.

107. **The Tales of Ise, attributed to Heian-era poets,** blends anonymous narratives with romantic poems, exploring love, adventure, and the impermanence of beauty.

108. **Artists developed their own styles, such as Yamato-e** (today considered the classical Japanese style of painting).

109. **Upper-class women had more intellectual freedom than before, with some even becoming famous poets such as Sei Shonagon.** It's important to remember that the vast majority of Japanese women had few, if any, rights well into the 20th century.

110. **Pure Land Buddhism, which was introduced to Japan in the 8th century,** developed into a widespread and popular form of Buddhism during the Heian era.

111. **Pure Land Buddhism emphasized devotion to Amitabha Buddha** (an ancient monk) and the aspiration to be reborn in his Pure Land, a realm of enlightenment and liberation.

112. **There were many important historical figures from this era, including Fujiwara no Michinaga,** who was one of Japan's most powerful politicians. He was from the Fujiwara clan, which controlled Japan behind the scenes in the imperial court in the 10th and 11th centuries.

113. **The Heian period also saw the development of complex court ceremonies** that set out rules for how people should behave **in front of the emperor** or other high-ranking officials.

114. **While no complete Heian-era castles remain, remnants and archaeological evidence tell their story.** At Fujiwara no Sumitomo's fortification (940s), earthworks and moats are visible, offering insights into Heian-era defensive structures.

115. **The Heian period also saw the development of a Japanese writing system called kana,** which uses syllables derived from Chinese characters.

116. **Kana refers to two syllabic scripts: hiragana and katakana. These scripts were developed as simplified versions of Chinese characters** (kanji) to represent native Japanese phonetic sounds.

117. **The Pillow Book is a classic work of Japanese literature written by court lady Sei Shonagon during the Heian period.** It is a collection of essays, anecdotes, observations, and reflections that offer a vivid and intimate glimpse into the daily life, thoughts, and experiences of aristocratic court society in Kyoto.

118. **A new type of music called Gagaku was developed during this time.** This musical style was influenced by Chinese court music.

119. **A famous example of Heian architecture is Byodo-in Temple, located near Kyoto.** Today, many visitors go there to admire the beautiful architecture and artwork from the Heian era.

120. **Toward the end of the Heian period, the Fujiwara clan became weak.** A struggle for power began between two large clans, **the Minamoto and the Taira,** and their allies. The struggle ended with **Minamoto no Yoritomo's victory over the Taira at Dan-no-Ura** in 1185.

Kamakura Period
(1185–1333)

This chapter will explore **the fascinating history of the Kamakura period.** We'll take a look at twenty interesting facts about this period, including **how Zen Buddhism flourished and the importance of the samurai.** We'll also discover how **the Japanese defeated Kublai Khan's Mongol invasion.** Explore the evolution of Japanese culture, and see why this period went down in the history books.

121. **The capital of Japan moved from Kyoto to Kamakura** (about forty miles southwest of modern-day Tokyo) during this period, hence the name. **Kamakura became an important political center** for many centuries after that.

122. **During this time, a new military government called the shogunate was established,** with Minamoto no Yoritomo as its first shogun, a political military leader.

123. **Yoritomo Minamoto had been raised within the Taira clan after his father's death in a battle.** However, he and his brothers were considered a threat and were exiled. During his exile, he built alliances and a military force that eventually allowed him to defeat the Taira.

124. **Zen Buddhism flourished in Japan during this time** and had a great impact on all aspects of Japanese culture, including art, architecture, literature, philosophy, and more.

125. **Zen Buddhism is a school of Mahayana Buddhism** that emphasizes direct experience and meditation as a means to achieve enlightenment. **It originated in China but was later introduced to Japan.**

126. **Kamakura-era samurai found Zen Buddhism deeply attractive.** Its focus on discipline, simplicity, and accepting hardship mirrored their values.

127. **A large number of samurai were retained by lords to protect their territory from other clans or invaders during this era.** A retainer is someone who holds and defends land for a lord in exchange for favor, power, treasure, or influence.

128. **Feudalism developed rapidly during this time.** Feudalism in Japan was somewhat similar to feudalism in western Europe at the time.

129. **The Kamakura period was a time of continued cultural exchange with China,** which brought new ideas to Japan, such as many new Buddhist principles.

130. **One of the most famous literary works from the Kamakura period is The Tale of the Heike** (Heike Monogatari), an epic narrative that chronicles the rise and fall of the Taira clan and the Genpei War between the Taira and Minamoto clans.

131. **In 1274 and again in 1281, Mongol leader Kublai Khan led an invasion of Japan but was defeated by the Japanese,** who were aided by two different typhoons. These typhoons destroyed many Mongol ships during the invasions.

132. **The Japanese call typhoons kamikaze** ("divine wind"). The term was coined during the 1281 Mongol invasion.

133. **Though many people believe that the storms ended the Mongol invasion before it even began,** Mongol troops did land in Japan, and costly battles did take place.

134. **During this time, Japan experienced a period of economic growth due to expanding trade with China and Korea,** which led to greater urbanization in some areas.

135. **During this period, Noh theater developed. Noh is a form of musical drama that combines masks,** music, dance, and chanting into a performance for entertainment or religious purposes.

136. **Noh is still performed today, but it is considered to be more of an upper-class entertainment like opera is in the West.**

137. **Poetry flourished during the Kamakura period. Renga** (linked verse) grew in popularity, and many famous poets were born during this era.

138. **During the Kamakura period, the samurai class gained prominence as the dominant military and social elite.** They served as the backbone of the shogunate's military forces and held key positions in the administration. This marked a transition from the previous aristocratic court culture to a society where military prowess and martial values held greater importance.

139. **Today, the city of Kamakura, which is about thirty-five miles southwest of Tokyo, attracts hundreds of thousands of tourists each year,** mostly because of its replica samurai villages, battle reenactments, and temples.

140. **The Kamakura period came to an end primarily due to internal conflicts and shifts in political power.** It ended in 1338 with the ascension of Ashikaga Takauji as shogun.

Muromachi Period
(1336–1573)

This chapter **will explore the Muromachi period in Japan, a time of strong military.** We'll take a look at twenty interesting facts about this era. Learn some captivating facts about **the Onin War, technology, art, and trade.**

141. **The Muromachi period** in Japan started in 1336 when **samurai lord Ashikaga Takauji became a dominant figure.** He was made shogun by the imperial court in 1338.

142. **The Muromachi period was a time of strong military rule.** Samurai warriors were very influential, as were powerful clans, such as the Takeda, Uesugi, Hojo, and Mori.

143. **Takauji wasn't initially a rebel. He was appointed a shogun by Emperor Go-Daigo,** whom he later helped overthrow, establishing his own Ashikaga shogunate.

144. **Takauji's feud with Go-Daigo's successor created two rival courts.** A complicated series of events ended with two rival families vying for control of Japan.

145. **Zen Buddhism became even more popular,** as did meditation practices called zazen used by samurai warriors.

146. Though **the Onin War** (1467–1477) **began as a localized conflict,** it spread and was eventually fought **between two factions within the court.** It destroyed much of central and western Japan.

147. **The Onin War marked the beginning of the rise in inter-clan warfare throughout Japan.** Though there were periods of peace, **Japan remained in a virtual state of war until 1600.**

148. **The formalized Japanese tea ceremony we recognize today emerged during the Muromachi period and became an important part of samurai culture** as a way to show respect to guests. It also incorporates elements of Zen meditation.

149. One of the most influential and popular books of the Ashikaga period is Tsurezuregusa, often translated as Essays in Idleness or The Harvest of Leisure. It was written by **the Japanese monk Yoshida Kenko** in the 1330s but remained exceedingly popular. It's considered a **classic of Japanese literature** and provides a glimpse into the mindset and culture of **the Muromachi** and later periods.

150. Architecture and interior design flourished with new styles being developed, such as the shoin style, which featured tatami mats, sliding doors, and shelves known as chigaidana.

151. Zen gardens or rock gardens became popular during the Muromachi period. They gave spaces a sense of tranquility and peace from all the wars going on in Japan.

152. Though there were many conflicts at this time, innovations did occur in art forms such as painting, calligraphy, and sculpture, resulting in some beautiful works being produced.

153. In 1543, **the first Europeans, Portuguese traders, arrived in Japan and introduced new goods, such as guns, tobacco, and distilled liquor,** as well as ideas like Christianity.

154. **The Muromachi period saw trade increase with China and Korea** due to increased stability after years of civil war between clans.

155. **Women had limited roles, but they managed to gain influence through their participation in arranged weddings and important ceremonies at court,** where they could showcase their skills, such as singing and dancing.

156. **Rice cultivation improved during this period,** allowing for more food production than ever before and leading to population growth throughout the country.

157. **This period saw the rise of haiku poetry and Noh theater,** which became popular forms of entertainment.

158. In 1568, **Oda Nobunaga began his campaign to unify Japan,** which ended up lasting until he died in 1582, when **Toyotomi Hideyoshi** took over, completing what is known as the unification of Japan.

159. In 1573, **warlord Oda Nobunaga sacked the city of Kyoto,** bringing an end to **the Muromachi period.**

160. **With the ascension of Nobunaga,** all of Japan was unified under one rule for the first time in its history.

Azuchi-Momoyama Period
(1573– 1600)

The Azuchi-Momoyama period was an era of great change in Japan, as the country was unified under one strong leader and saw advances in commerce and industry. **During this period, castles were built across Japan, samurai were given increased rights,** and tea ceremonies became more popular. Let's take a look at twenty interesting facts about this captivating period that shaped Japanese society.

161. The Azuchi-Momoyama period was a time of great change in Japan, as the country was unified under one strong leader, first under **Oda Nobunaga** and then **Toyotomi Hideyoshi.**

162. In 1573, **the warlord Oda Nobunaga captured Kyoto,** the capital. Nobunaga did not assume the title of shogun for many reasons. Instead, he ruled behind the scenes.

163. Nobunaga is considered the first of the three "Great Unifiers" of Japan.

164. **Nobunaga moved his headquarters to Azuchi Castle on Lake Biwa near Kyoto** in 1576, thus giving this period its name, **"Azuchi-Momoyama."**

165. **In addition to Japan becoming unified politically,** other big changes during this period included advances in commerce and industry, such as the increased use of firearms and mining techniques.

166. In 1582, **Nobunaga was assassinated by his former ally and general, Akechi Mitsuhide,** after having begun to reunify the country.

167. By the end of this period, **hundreds of castles had been built across Japan;** some famous castles include **Osaka Castle and Kumamoto Castle.**

168. **The samurai class was given increased rights and privileges during this period. The samurai only accounted for between 7 and 10 percent of the population at the time,** but they had all the power.

169. **Samurai were allowed to wear bright colors, which set them apart from the commoners,** who had to dress in duller tones, such as black or gray.

170. **Tea ceremonies blossomed during the Azuchi-Momoyama period.** These ceremonies became a popular way for high-ranking people to show off their wealth and power. They hosted elaborate gatherings with expensive imported Chinese wares.

171. **One of Nobunaga's generals was Toyotomi Hideyoshi,** whose talent and ambition allowed him to enter the samurai class. **Hideyoshi brought about Akechi Mitsuhide's downfall and became kampaku or chief advisor to the emperor,** a position he held from 1585 to 1592.

172. **Hideyoshi could not become a shogun because of his peasant background.**

173. **Toyotomi Hideyoshi became a major patron of the arts and architecture.**

174. **The Azuchi-Momoyama period saw a rise in trade with other countries, which brought new goods like tobacco, sugar cane, and potatoes to Japan.** The Europeans started to come to Japan in greater numbers in the 1500s.

175. **In 1588, Toyotomi Hideyoshi ordered his famous "sword hunt." He banned people from owning edged weapons** (the samurai could still own them, though). This was an attempt to reduce violence, maintain order, and reduce the chances of a peasant uprising against samurai rule.

176. By 1603, **over three million people were living in Japan,** making it one of the most densely populated countries in East Asia at that time.

177. **The first official Japanese diplomatic mission to Europe wasn't until 1582.** Daimyo Ōtomo Sōrin sent the Tenshō embassy, which was officially received by European rulers. This mission sought both religious dialogue and the establishment of trade and political ties.

178. The economy flourished throughout **Nobunaga's** rule. Merchants, though looked down upon socially, started to amass wealth. Nobunaga promoted international trade.

179. When Hideyoshi died in 1598, **there was a power vacuum in Japan, with many clans fighting for control.**

180. After Nobunaga died in 1582, **Toyotomi Hideyoshi** dominated, but he faced challenges from Tokugawa Ieyasu, **Nobunaga's former general.** Though initially allied with **Hideyoshi's** son, Ieyasu decisively defeated both forces at **Sekigahara** in 1600. Through complex maneuvers, peace was secured, paving the way for Ieyasu's shogunate.

Edo Period
(1603–1867)

The Edo period was a time of great cultural and political developments in Japan. During this period, movement around the country was restricted to keep order while culture flourished. **There were advances in military technology, and literacy rates increased.** We'll explore all this while taking a look at twenty-five interesting facts about this period that shaped modern Japanese society.

181. **The Edo period, also known as the Tokugawa period,** began in 1603 when **Tokugawa Ieyasu became the shogun of Japan** and lasted until 1867.

182. During this period, Japan was divided into around three hundred feudal domains ruled by powerful local lords called daimyo, who were loyal to the shogun.

183. **The shogun ruled in the name of the emperor.** By this time, the emperor was just a figurehead.

184. In 1635, **the Sakoku Edict was enacted. "Sakoku" means "closed country" or "isolationist policy,"** and the edict forbade all Japanese from traveling abroad. It also limited foreigners, mostly Europeans, to a small area in the southern port city of Hiroshima, with few exceptions.

185. **Breaking the Sakoku Edict was punishable by death. Japan** entered an era of two hundred years of virtual isolation from the rest of the world.

186. **Because of the edict, no new foreign ideas or technologies came into Japan.** So, when the isolation policy ended in the mid-19th century, Japan was two hundred years behind much of the world, particularly Europe and America.

187. **In much of Japan, travel was heavily restricted, especially for non-samurai.** Permits were often needed, checkpoints were everywhere, and travel taxes and tolls were imposed.

188. **Buddhism was still an important part of life in the Edo period,** but Shintoism started gaining popularity again due to its focus on Japanese traditions and reverence for the emperor.

189. **The Edo period was marked by an increase in literacy,** especially among the merchant class, which grew in power and influence as the Edo period went by.

190. **Cities like Edo (modern-day Tokyo) grew quickly.** They became important trade centers, where large markets would be filled with goods from around the country and sometimes even abroad.

191. **A popular form of entertainment during this period was kabuki,** plays where actors dressed up in elaborate costumes to tell stories about love, war, and other topics through music, dance, and dialogue.

192. **Kabuki was more popular with the common people and lower-ranked samurai than those at the top.**

193. **In kabuki, the female roles were played by male actors.** Having women act was considered too provocative for the public.

194. **Sumo wrestling became increasingly popular among ordinary people,** who enjoyed watching it at tournaments held in local towns across Japan.

195. **In southern Japan, Christianity began to take hold with a growing portion of the population.** The religion had grown slowly with the arrival of the Europeans in the early 1500s.

196. **Though some samurai lords became Christian,** most, including the shoguns, saw it as a threat.

197. **During the Shimabara Rebellion in southern Japan, from 1637 to 1638, the government began a violent persecution of Christians,** resulting in tens of thousands of deaths and driving the religion underground.

198. **Samurai warriors were still important members of society,** though their role had changed from fighting battles on the battlefield to mainly governance and law enforcement.

199. **Toward the end of the Edo period, much of the samurai class had become idle.** Many developed gambling and alcohol problems stemming from idleness and the loss of power.

200. **The Edo period saw advances in military technology,** with guns becoming increasingly popular among samurai, though they did not replace swords entirely.

201. **Gun technology came from the Europeans, mainly the Dutch, who were the preferred trading partners of the bakufu, or "big tent," as the government was referred to.** The term refers to early shoguns holding court and hearings in a big tent. The word has come to mean shogunate today.

202. **During this time, a system called han, or "domain," school was set up.** Children from wealthy families could receive education suited to their social class, while poorer children received little or no formal schooling at all.

203. In 1682, **a law was passed that required every household throughout Japan to register with its local government office** so that it would be easier for authorities to keep track of people who lived there or visited from other parts of the country.

204. **By the end of the Edo period, around half of all Japanese people lived in cities, making Japan one of the most urbanized countries at that time.**

205. T**he last shogun, Tokugawa Yoshinobu,** resigned in 1867, which marked an end to both the Edo period and the Tokugawa shogunate.

End of Isolation and the Meiji Restoration
(1853–1912)

The Meiji Restoration was a period of great change in Japan as the country began to modernize. During this time, **Emperor Meiji introduced reforms to replace old feudal land systems with private ownership,** increased people's freedoms and rights regardless of social status or wealth, revamped the education system, and opened up Japan to foreign influence through trade and diplomatic relations. We'll explore all this through twenty interesting facts.

206. In 1853, **and again the next year, a powerful American naval fleet arrived in Japan.** Refusing to go away until the country opened up to trade, the American visit ended Japan's isolation policy.

207. In 1868, **Emperor Meiji took the throne, beginning the period known as the Meiji Restoration.**

208. **The goal of this period was to modernize and industrialize Japan** so it could catch up to the Western powers, protect its independence, and eventually become a powerful modern country.

209. **One of the first reforms made during this time was to replace old feudal land systems** with a new system based on private ownership called kazoku seido (noble family system).

210. **The samurai class lost their privileges and special rights under the new government** but were given pensions for their service to the empire.

211. **New laws were introduced that allowed people more freedom and equal rights regardless of social status or wealth level;** these included the outlawing of slavery-like practices such as debt bondage and forced labor contracts, among other things.

212. **The education system underwent significant changes. Primary school became compulsory for all children,** and higher learning institutions expanded throughout the country, offering courses in science, mathematics, literature, philosophy, and more.

213. **During this period, Japan opened its doors to foreign influence and ideas,** which helped it progress rapidly in technology, industry, and military strength. **Railways were built all over the country,** and telegraph lines connected cities.

214. **From 1868 to 1869, there was a civil war called the Boshin War.** The conflict was between forces supporting the shogunate and those wanting a restoration of imperial rule. **The imperial side won, leading to the enthronement of Emperor Meiji.**

215. From 1894 to 1895, **Japan fought a war with China, known as the First Sino-Japanese War, over control of Korea.** The Japanese won decisively after just six months and took over Korea and Taiwan, the latter of which was called **Formosa**.

216. From 1904 to 1905, **Japan fought against Russia for influence in the Pacific and Korea.** In the **Russo-Japanese War,** Japanese forces again emerged victorious, securing Japan's place on the international stage for good.

217. **During this time, Japan became the first East Asian country to have a written constitution,** which included provisions for some popular representation in government.

218. **This period saw an expansion of the Japanese Empire across Asia.** Japan took control of Korea, Taiwan, and parts of China, setting up puppet governments in these regions to secure its rule.

219. **The Meiji era was responsible for sparking cultural revolutions,** such as creating new art movements and a renewed interest in Shintoism.

220. In 1912, **Emperor Meiji passed away,** bringing about the end of his reign and the restoration project that had modernized Japan considerably.

221. **The death of the emperor marked the official start of the Taisho period** (named for Emperor Taisho), where further reforms were introduced.

222. **In Japan, there are two types of calendars: the Western calendar,** which is used throughout the world, and the imperial calendar. The imperial calendar resets with the death of an emperor.

223. **The emperor is given a posthumous name that describes his reign. Emperor Meiji's real name was Mutsuhito.** He was only called Meiji, which means "enlightened rule," after his death.

224. **One of the new inventions that fascinated Japan was the steam train.** A miniature steam train was given to the Japanese as a gift from the US. **The Japanese reverse-engineered** it to gain an understanding of the technology.

225. **Under Emperor Meiji's rule, many foreign ideas, such as the introduction of Western clothing styles,** were incorporated into Japanese culture.

Taisho Period
(1912–1926)

The Taisho period was a time of great change in Japan. It saw an economic boom, a massive earthquake, and advances in education. Here are twenty interesting facts about this engaging era.

226. **The Taisho period began in 1912 and ended in 1926.**

227. **Emperor Taisho (Yoshihito) was the 123rd emperor of Japan. Yoshihito** was mentally challenged to a degree. Powerful figures, mostly from old samurai families, ruled in his name.

228. **During the early years of the Taisho period,** Japan experienced a great economic boom with increased production and consumption across all industries and classes.

229. **In 1914, World War I began. Japan joined the Allies and fought a number of small battles against German forces in China and the Pacific.** At the end of World War I, Japan received control of many German territories in China and the Pacific.

230. **There was an increase in publications, films, radio broadcasts, and music recordings,** which brought Western culture into everyday Japanese life.

231. **More people had access to education, which led to more civil rights awareness among citizens,** including women's rights movements like suffrage campaigns for political representation and labor movements for better working conditions.

232. **The government passed several laws, such as compulsory education acts that extended educational opportunities,** making them available even to those from lower socioeconomic backgrounds.

233. **In 1916, the first nationwide election took place, allowing people to vote for their local representatives.** Women could not vote at this time.

234. **By 1918, baseball was one of the most popular sports in Japan.** Its popularity continued to grow throughout the 20th century.

235. **In 1923, an earthquake known as the Great Kanto Earthquake shook Tokyo, killing more than 100,000 people.** The death toll was so high because much of Tokyo was built with wood. Fire destroyed much of the city.

236. **The year 1923 saw a surge of nationalism, leading to popular support for military expansion in Asia and other regions.** This nationalism grew into a unique type of fascism by the mid-1930s.

237. **In 1924, the General Election Law was passed,** which allowed all men over twenty-five years of age to have voting rights regardless of property or social status.

238. Japan joined the League of Nations in 1920. **The League's main purpose was international peacekeeping efforts,** but the League of Nations ultimately failed for many reasons. Japan quit the League in 1933 after the organization condemned its annexation of Manchuria.

239. **In both Japan and the US, military men began planning for what they saw as an inevitable war between the two countries. Japan was expanding into China,** an American ally, and into the Pacific. America had territories all over the Pacific, including the colony of the Philippines.

240. **In the peace agreement signed with Russia, Japan gained Russian territory in southern Manchuria,** including the industrialized Kwantung Peninsula on the coast. This would later be the springboard for Japan's invasion of the rest of Manchuria in the 1930s.

241. **The period also brought about the Taisho culture, which included art movements such as shin-hanga and literature,** including fiction novels and tankas or poems by renowned authors like Jun'ichiro Tanizaki.

242. **In the 1920s, Japan, like many countries around the world, experienced an invasion of American culture, including movies, clothing, sports, dance, and much else.** Many people loved the new things coming to Japan, but many did not.

243. **There was a growth in consumerism, with increased production of items from food products to clothing brands. Japan also received imports from other parts of the world, especially America and Europe.**

244. By 1926, **Japan had become an industrial powerhouse. The country produced cars,** refined steel, and even created ships for export.

245. **This era ended when Emperor Hirohito ascended the throne, ushering in the Showa era.**

Showa Period
(1926–1989)

The Showa period marked a time of rapid advancement in Japan. During this period, Japan experienced the highs of hosting the Summer Olympics and the lows of natural disasters like earthquakes. Explore twenty interesting facts about this fascinating period that shaped Japanese society for generations to come.

246. The Showa period began in 1926 when Emperor Hirohito took the throne after his father's death.

247. **This period was a time of rapid industrialization and economic growth for Japan,** with new technology being used to develop things like radios and cars.

248. **In 1931, Japan invaded Manchuria (in China), starting World War II in Asia** before it began in Europe in 1939.

249. **During WWII, many Japanese fought on battlefields around the world.** Some even volunteered as kamikaze suicide pilots during wartime battles between 1944 and 1945.

250. In 1945, Japan surrendered, ending World War II. Allied forces occupied the country until 1952.

251. During this time, democracy was introduced to Japan as part of a wide-ranging program of political reforms imposed by the United States.

252. By the late 1950s, **there was a huge surge in Japanese manufacturing and exports,** which led to increased wealth for many people living there at this time.

253. **Most manufacturing at this time was of smaller, cheaper consumer goods.** In the 1960s, Japan began to produce heavier manufacturing products like cars, trucks, and ships.

254. **The Japanese economic miracle began in the 1960s.** Japan achieved one of the highest economic growth rates in world history.

255. **The 1964 Summer Olympics were hosted by Tokyo, symbolically bringing Japan back into the community of nations after its aggressive role in WWII.**

256. In 1964, **a powerful earthquake struck Niigata Prefecture. The quake caused widespread destruction,** with over 3,500 houses demolished and 11,000 damaged. While the death toll from the quake remained relatively low, a tsunami triggered by the earthquake further impacted coastal areas.

257. **During this period, major advances were made in science and technology, with Nobel Prizes awarded to Japanese scientists for their work on lasers** (1985) and superconductivity (1987).

258. In 1972, **Emperor Hirohito visited China, marking an important step toward better relations between the two countries after WWII.** In 1975, Hirohito made a controversial visit to the US, its prime enemy during WWII.

259. The late 1970s **saw a rise in political awareness among young people who wanted more freedom from the government** and better control over their lives.

260. In 1982, **a giant Japanese corporation, Sony, released its first compact disc player,** ushering in a new era of music consumption around the world.

261. **In 1985, the Japanese National Railways were privatized and divided into several regional rail companies,** leading to a more efficient national railway system.

262. **Japan has had one of the world's most modern rail systems for decades.** Japan developed the world's first "bullet train" in 1964.

263. **The Showa period ended in 1989 when Emperor Hirohito passed away after ruling Japan for sixty-two years.** He had the longest rule in Japanese history.

264. **This period birthed some of Japan's most beloved anime series, such as Astro Boy** (1963) and **Mobile Suit Gundam** (1979).

265. **In 1986, Nintendo released its first home video game console, which became an instant hit with people around the world.**

Japan in World War II

By 1936, power in Japan was in the hands of the military. Generals and admirals planned for a war of expansion into Asia and the Pacific with the aim of forming a "ring" around Japan to expand Japanese control and influence and "protect" it from Western elements. Let's take a look at twenty interesting facts about Japan's actions during World War II.

266. Japan's invasion of China in 1936 marked the beginning of its militaristic expansion in Asia.

267. **Japan's war with China intensified with the Marco Polo Bridge Incident in 1937,** leading to a full-scale conflict.

268. In 1940, Japan allied with Nazi Germany and fascist Italy, forming the Axis Powers.

269. **The US imposed an embargo on Japan, including oil and steel,** in response to its expansionist actions in Asia. Facing economic hardships due to the embargo, Japan began planning for military action in the Pacific

270. **On December 7th, 1941, Japan launched a surprise attack on the US naval base at Pearl Harbor,** leading to America's entry into WWII.

271. **Though the attack on Pearl Harbor was a surprise, many leading politicians and military** officials in both nations expected war between the two countries since the 1920s.

272. **During the war, Japan rapidly expanded in Asia and the Pacific, capturing territories like Hong Kong, Singapore, the Philippines, and the Dutch East Indies.**

273. **The Battle of Midway in June 1942 was a turning point in the war,** halting Japan's advance and weakening its naval forces.

274. **Japanese forces committed numerous war crimes in China, such as the Nanking Massacre and the use of chemical weapons.**

275. **The Allies adopted an "island-hopping" strategy,** bypassing heavily fortified Japanese-held islands and capturing strategically important ones.

276. In 1944, **the US captured the Mariana Islands,** gaining air bases that allowed Allied soldiers to launch long-range bombing raids on Japan.

277. Japanese kamikaze pilots used suicide attacks with aircraft to inflict damage on Allied ships.

278. **The Battle of Iwo Jima and the Battle of Okinawa were fierce conflicts that foreshadowed the challenges of an invasion of Japan's main islands.** Both battles highlighted the willingness of the Japanese to die rather than surrender. Those who didn't die in action often committed suicide in fortified caves built on the islands.

279. **On August 6th, 1945, the US dropped an atomic bomb on Hiroshima, leading to unprecedented devastation and loss of life.** Three days later, a second atomic bomb was dropped on Nagasaki, further accelerating Japan's decision to surrender.

280. On August 15th, 1945, **Emperor Hirohito announced Japan's surrender, effectively ending WWII.**

281. **Hirohito made the announcement over the radio, and it was the first time that his voice had been heard by the majority of the Japanese people.** Traditionally, the emperor's voice was only heard by his family, advisors, and in governmental meetings.

282. **The formal surrender ceremony took place aboard the USS Missouri in Tokyo Bay.** The Allied nations celebrated V-J Day (Victory over Japan Day).

283. **The International Military Tribunal for the Far East** (known as the Tokyo Trials) was held to prosecute Japanese war criminals.

284. **Though a number of leading Japanese, like former Prime Minister Tojo and General Yamashita,** were found guilty and executed, many others were never brought to justice.

285. **The Treaty of San Francisco of 1951 officially ended the war and allowed Japan to regain its sovereignty,** marking the beginning of its post-war reconstruction.

Post–World War II Japan
(1945–Present)

Since 1945, **Japan has enjoyed fast economic growth, technological advancements, and rising living standards.** These twenty intriguing facts will examine how these developments have molded Japan into one of the strongest global economies today.

286. **The United States occupied Japan from 1945 to 1952,** during which time a new constitution was written that included civil rights, such as the freedom of speech and the freedom of assembly.

287. **During this period, women were allowed to vote for the first time in Japanese history.**

288. **Shintoism was separated from politics to promote religious freedom among citizens.** During the 1930s and 1940s, Shintoism was sponsored and supported by the state, and people were subtly forced to attend Shinto services and donate money.

289. **After the US occupation ended in 1952, Japan experienced rapid economic growth.** This period is known as the Japanese economic miracle. This was due largely to industrialization efforts led by **Prime Minister Ikeda Hayato** between 1958 and 1964, which resulted in improved living standards across all classes of society.

290. In 1970, **novelist Yukio Mishima, revered for his work despite being a controversial figure, felt Japan had abandoned its traditional spirit.** Anguished by Westernization and yearning for a return to pre-war values, he took his own life in a dramatic act of protest.

291. In 1972, **Japan regained control over the Ryukyu Islands, which included Okinawa, and became a member of the United Nations.**

292. **Japan hosted Expo '85 to celebrate the anniversary of the first World's Fair held in 1851.** This event is credited with contributing significantly to the development of the country's modern tourism industry.

293. **From 1986 to 1991, Japan experienced a bubble where stock prices soared above their real values.** This economic bubble eventually burst, leading to a recession during the 1990s.

294. **By the late 1990s, digital technology had improved across all industries,** resulting in increased global exports for Japanese businesses, including cars, video games, electronics, and more.

295. **The 2002 World Cup was co-hosted by South Korea and Japan.** Both countries built stadiums and invested significant resources in the event, demonstrating the strength of their economies.

296. **In 2008, Japan became the first country to send an unmanned mission to the moon since 1976.**

297. The 2011 **Tohoku earthquake and tsunami caused widespread destruction in the northern part of Honshu Island,** resulting in over fifteen thousand deaths and numerous nuclear reactor meltdowns at the Fukushima Daiichi Nuclear Power Plant.

298. **In 1972, the northern city of Sapporo hosted the Winter Olympics. Tokyo was selected as the host city for the 2020 Summer Olympics;** this was the second time that the city hosted **the Summer Games** (the first one being the 1964 Olympics).

299. **On June 16th, 2013, Abe Shinzo** (known in the West as Shinzo Abe) assumed office and implemented economic policies known as **"Abenomics,"** which sought to stimulate a stagnant economy through increased government spending and quantitative easing, which involves low interest rates and an increase in the money supply.

300. In 2019, **Emperor Naruhito ascended the throne, starting the Reiwa era.** His father, Akihito, abdicated due to his advanced age, marking a historic shift in Japanese monarchy.

301. In June 2020, **the Japanese government passed the digital technology strategy**, which sought to promote the digitization of the economy and create new jobs within the tech industry through tax incentives and investments in new infrastructure.

302. **Compared to the US, Japan boasts remarkably low crime rates.** It is not known for sure why this is, but it likely involves strong social cohesion, efficient law enforcement, strict gun control, and a cultural emphasis on respect and conformity.

303. **Japan's booming youth culture, expressed through vibrant fashion trends and unique subcultures,** is often seen as a rebellion against tradition.

304. **Japan consumes roughly 80 percent of the world's bluefin tuna.** The price of the best bluefin tuna can vary greatly depending on factors like size, quality, and auction setting. In January 2023, the winning bid for a 212-kilogram bluefin tuna reached about $275,000 USD, which translates to roughly $1,300 per kilogram or $2,866 per pound.

305. **Though largely absent in daily life, kimonos still grace Japanese women on special occasions. Brides, graduates, and mourners don them for formal events,** while tea ceremonies, performances, and festivals offer glimpses of tradition.

The Japanese Constitution of 1947

The Japanese Constitution of 1947 is a document that has had an immense impact on the nation since its enactment. This chapter will explore the impressive history and lasting legacy of this important document.

306. **The Japanese Constitution was written in 1947 to replace the previous Meiji Constitution from 1889.**

307. **Its framework was written to a large degree by an American official named Courtney Whitney and his staff,** who worked under General Douglas MacArthur.

308. **The Japanese Constitution is considered one of the most pacifist constitutions due to its Article 9,** which renounces war and prohibits Japan from having a standing military force or participating in any wars outside of self-defense purposes.

309. **Article 9 is still intact today. It has faced criticism over the years, especially during the War on Terror,** when Japan was criticized for its lack of military involvement.

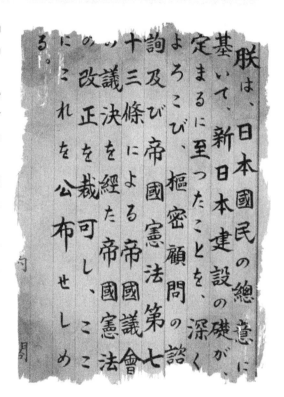

310. **Prime Minister Abe Shinzo attempted to revise the wording related to Article 9 in 2015** but failed due to strong opposition from some political parties in the Diet.

311. **The article remains a source of pride for many Japanese,** who view it as symbolizing their commitment to peace and human rights across the world today.

312. **Many point to American military protection for the lack of a need for a large amount of military spending,** though the Japanese have recently begun a military build-up to offset dangers from China.

313. **The Japanese Constitution guarantees the fundamental human rights of all citizens,** such as freedom of speech, religion, and assembly, as well as equality before the law, regardless of race or gender.

314. **The constitution introduced a parliamentary form of government, with an elected lower house** (the Diet) holding significant power over laws and budgets while giving more autonomy to local governments through decentralization efforts.

315. **Other notable features of the Japanese Constitution include the separation between religion and the state,** the prohibition of discrimination based on birth or social standing, and the right of individuals to work without exploitation or fear from employers.

316. **The Japanese Constitution has never been amended since its enactment despite many attempts over the years.** A two-thirds majority is required for any amendments.

317. **There have been several attempts to amend the Japanese Constitution over the years,** but they have all failed due to insufficient majority approval from both houses of the Diet and political infighting between different parties.

318. **The Japanese Constitution has been used as a model for many countries** seeking to build their own constitutions, including South Korea.

319. **Scholars suggest that Japan's post-war constitution,** which granted more freedoms than the people had before World War II, helped promote economic growth and stability.

320. **The Japanese Constitution is considered one of the longest-lasting post-war constitutions.**

Japan's Economic Miracle of the 1950s and Onward

The 1950s marked a period of great change in Japan, as the country transitioned from an agricultural-based economy to one of the world's most powerful industrialized nations. **In this chapter, we'll explore twenty interesting facts about Japan's economic miracle.**

321. **After World War II,** Japan was in ruins and faced extreme economic hardship.

322. **The Japanese government, in concert with the United States,** made an effort to rebuild the country's economy starting in 1950 with an export-oriented growth strategy. **This was the beginning of what is now known in Japanese history** as the economic miracle.

323. **This period marked Japan's transition from being primarily dependent on agriculture** to becoming one of the world's most powerful industrialized nations by 1970.

324. In 1953, **Japan entered into a trade agreement with America** that increased exports significantly and sparked more investment opportunities within the country as well as abroad.

325. **By 1960, steel production had quadrupled since 1950, when it was barely five million tons annually.**

326. **In 1966, Japan became one of the thirty-one original members of the Asian Development Bank (ADB),** helping provide funds for large-scale industrial projects that helped push their economic miracle further.

327. **In the early 1960s, Japan began to lift some of the post-war restrictions on foreign investment.** It also created a domestic policy that directed and encouraged economic expansion for the next decade.

328. **By 1965, Japanese companies had become a major presence in world markets,** with around one-fourth of all exports coming from Japan.

329. **The 1970s marked an even larger push for technological development by introducing new products,** such as color television sets, digital cameras, and VCRs, to international consumers.

330. **The rise of Japan's nuclear energy industry began in the 1950s, fueled by economic needs and post-war fear subsiding.** Peaceful developments under the Non-Proliferation Treaty saw rapid research and plant construction, making Japan a leader by the 1970s. However, **Fukushima's 2011 disaster drastically changed the landscape,** leaving many reactors offline and the industry's future in question.

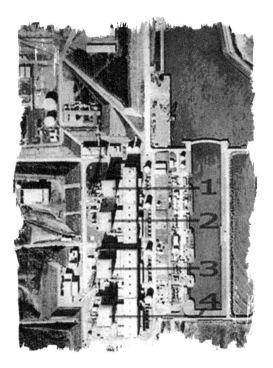

331. The 1975 **absorption of the Osaka and Nagoya exchanges by the Tokyo Stock Exchange cemented its status as a global financial powerhouse,** not just a regional leader.

332. **During this period, large-scale manufacturing projects were initiated, like the petrochemical complex at Kawasaki City and Nissan's Zama plant,** where automobile production increased drastically.

333. By 1980, **Japanese car manufacturers were making cars in both Japan and the United States.**

334. **The 1980s saw technologies, such as personal computers,** which quickly became popular among Japanese consumers.

335. **In 1985, the Plaza Accord was signed with other world leaders that allowed Japan's currency,** the yen, to appreciate against the US dollar and European currencies, helping boost exports.

336. **By 1990, Japan had become one of the most powerful economies in the world,** contributing more than 10 percent to the global GDP (gross domestic product).

337. **In 1992, the improvement of bullet trains helped further boost productivity by allowing people to travel faster between cities like Tokyo and Osaka** during peak hours at speeds up to three hundred kilometers an hour.

338. **The 2000s saw the emergence of digital technologies like smartphones, tablets, and laptops,** giving Japanese citizens access to modern communication devices.

339. **Today, Japan is a major economic powerhouse in Asia and the world,** with one of the highest GDP per capita rates in the world.

340. **Since 1975, Japanese food and culture have exploded globally. Anime, manga, and video games sparked interest in the Japanese lifestyle.** Sushi, ramen, and other unique flavors tantalized taste buds, while pop culture trends fueled a fascination with Japanese fashion, music, and design.

Japanese Oil Crisis
(1973)

The Japanese oil crisis saw the country face skyrocketing oil prices. We'll explore this crisis through twenty interesting facts about **Japan's economic, political, and social changes.**

341. **In 1973, the Japanese oil crisis began when Arab members of the Organization of Petroleum Exporting Countries** (OPEC) decided to severely limit oil exports to Japan in protest against their support for Israel during a war in the Middle East.

342. **The embargo on oil from OPEC caused prices to skyrocket, and supplies quickly ran out across Japan.** Japan produces almost zero petroleum itself and has to import it.

343. **To deal with this crisis, Japan started rationing gas and fuel, limiting business hours so that people would use less energy,** encouraging carpools, and asking people not to drive except for essential trips, such as going to work or school.

344. **Prime Minister Tanaka Kakuei Tanaka asked citizens to conserve energy in 1974,** causing many changes, such as closing railway stations early and turning off street lights after midnight.

345. **During this period, there was an increase in electric bicycles and bicycle sales throughout Japan.**

346. **In 1974, the Japanese government passed a law that allowed companies to produce cars with smaller engines, which became known as "kei" cars.** These cars used less fuel than regular models. **The first Honda export to the US, the N600,** got between thirty-six to forty miles per gallon, which was amazing for the time.

347. **The crisis led to an increase in the development of alternative sources of energy,** including solar, geothermal, and nuclear power plants.

348. **Since Japan had become so reliant on oil from OPEC countries,** it was forced to look for different suppliers, such as Australia, Mexico, and Canada, which could provide the Japanese with crude oil at lower prices.

349. **During this crisis, there was an increased emphasis placed on research into renewable energy sources,** such as wind and wave power, along with other forms of clean energy technology like hydrogen-cell vehicles.

350. **Many people embraced traditional methods of transportation during this time,** including human-powered boats for fishing trips or hauling goods across water routes instead of using motorized ships powered by fossil fuels.

351. **Japan responded to the oil crisis with immediate conservation efforts, diversification of energy sources, and stockpiling.** Longer-term strategies included industrial restructuring, technological advancements, and diplomatic efforts, ultimately leading to a more resilient and energy-efficient economy.

352. **During this time, there was an increased emphasis placed on recycling materials** and encouraging citizens to create compost piles for their gardens or homes.

353. **The energy crisis highlighted Japan's continued dependence on the United States.** Though the US was also affected by the actions of OPEC, US naval forces ensured open shipping lanes in the Middle East, allowing oil to flow to Japan and elsewhere.

354. **The Japanese oil crisis saw huge advances made in terms of public transportation, including devising efficient railway networks** that could transport passengers quickly and efficiently despite having limited resources available due to fuel shortages.

355. **After the oil embargo ended in 1974,** prices slowly returned but didn't reach pre-crisis levels until 1978.

356. **Along with cultural and geographical issues, the Japanese began making even more cars to export to the US.** These cars far outgained US models in miles per gallon for decades.

357. **Following this crisis, Japanese citizens were encouraged to use more efficient lighting,** such as LED bulbs instead of traditional incandescent ones, or to buy more fuel-efficient cars rather than those that guzzled petrol.

358. **The Japanese government increased its focus on nuclear power following the OPEC oil crisis of the 1970s.** The crisis highlighted Japan's heavy dependence on imported oil for energy, which led to concerns about energy security.

359. **After the oil crisis, Japan embarked on a program to expand its nuclear power capacity.** This led to the construction of several nuclear power stations in the years following **the OPEC crisis.**

360. **Due to their experience with this oil crisis, many Japanese companies have continued to invest in and develop new energy sources,** such as fuel cells, solar panels, wind turbines, and other green technologies.

The 1980s Bubble Economy

This chapter will explore the events of the Japanese Bubble Economy, from how it began to its eventual end and its impact on Japan today. We'll look at twenty interesting facts about what life was like during these five years.

361. **In the 1980s, Japan experienced a period of economic growth now called the Bubble Economy.** This period was created by banks and businesses giving out large amounts of loans, which raised stock prices and caused property values to rise rapidly.

362. **During this time, Japanese citizens had more money than ever before to spend on things like electronics or luxury goods.** They were some of the wealthiest people in the world.

363. **By 1989, Japan's economy made up over 17 percent of the entire global GDP.**

364. **Since there were so many investments going into different industries, Japanese companies** were able to expand their products all over the world. Cars like **Honda and Toyota** became popular everywhere.

365. **During the economic bubble, property values in Tokyo were significantly higher than those in New York City.** Tokyo experienced a property bubble characterized by soaring real estate prices and excessive speculation.

366. **At its peak, the value of some prime real estate in Tokyo,** such as the grounds of the Imperial Palace, exceeded the value of all real estate in California.

367. **Japanese citizens started to invest in more and more assets, such as stocks, real estate, and art, causing the prices of these items to skyrocket.** These investments were not based on the health or strength of companies. People wanted to "get rich quick."

368. **The government put a lot of money into public works projects during this time,** which boosted the economy even further.

369. **In order to keep up with the rapid growth, businesses had to take on larger amounts of debt,** making them vulnerable if the Bubble Economy ever stopped growing or crashed, which it eventually did.

370. **By 1990, it became clear that Japan's economic growth was slowing significantly.** Stock prices began dropping, and property values declined quickly.

371. **Millions of people lost their life savings.** Many lost great fortunes.

372. **Many businesses were unable to pay back their loans**, which led banks and other financial institutions to face serious losses, leading them toward bankruptcy.

373. **With so much economic uncertainty, people started saving instead of spending,** causing consumption levels within Japan to drop dramatically.

374. **As the economy started to recover, banks and businesses** had to change their policies to ensure that investments were safer and more secure.

375. **The Japanese government implemented stricter regulations on loans** and made it harder for companies to expand too quickly, preventing another "Bubble Economy" from happening again.

376. Despite all this, by 1996, **the Japanese economy was beginning to slowly grow again,** though it took time and didn't trickle down to many individuals until much later.

377. **One of the signs of the economy's collapse was a growth in homelessness,** especially among the elderly, some of whom lost pensions overnight.

378. **In Tokyo, subway stations were used to sleep in during the night** and early morning hours when few people were around.

379. **Although there are still debates about whether or not another "Bubble Economy" could happen in Japan,** experts agree that any future economic growth must be sustainable and avoid risky investments like those seen during this period.

380. **To commemorate the thirtieth anniversary of the end of the bubble era** (in 2021), many museums throughout Japan held exhibitions and events to help educate people about what happened during this time.

Japan's Lost Decade
(the 1990s)

This chapter will explore the economic crisis that plagued Japan in the 1990s, otherwise known as the Lost Decade. We'll take a look at twenty interesting facts about this period, including the major causes of this downturn.

381. **During Japan's Lost Decade, the country's economy generally stagnated.** It started in 1991 and lasted until around 2001.

382. **In 1989, Japanese stocks hit their highest peak ever at 38,915 points on the Nikkei Stock** Average index (the main stock market for Japan).

383. By 1992, **the Nikkei had dropped to 14,309 points,** almost two-thirds lower than its peak only three years earlier.

384. **The collapse of real estate prices, mostly caused by an inability to repay loans due to inflated prices,** was one of the key causes of this economic downturn in Japan.

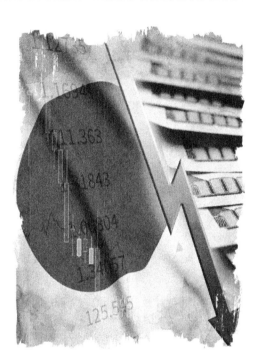

385. **Banks were also affected by bad loans made during Japan's property bubble,** which burst in 1991, leading to an increase in non-performing loan ratios (essentially loans that were not being paid back).

386. **This recession caused massive unemployment rates,** with millions of people losing their jobs between 1993 and 1995 alone.

387. **One of the tough choices that large companies had to make at this time was whether to change the lifetime employment that was virtually guaranteed to their workers.** Unfortunately, most of the people "let go" were older workers who had more difficulty finding employment.

388. **Despite these efforts, GDP growth in Japan was still negative** from 1992 to 1997 and only started to turn positive again in 1998.

389. **Japan's booming 1980s gave way to the harsh realities of the Lost Decade.** The economic decline pushed many people deeper into poverty, with job losses and wage stagnation eroding living standards.

390. **During this period, many Japanese companies had to restructure or go bankrupt** due to a decrease in demand for their goods and services, which caused massive layoffs.

391. **To improve its economy, Japan's central bank decreased interest rates to encourage people to take out loans for investments** in large and small businesses. This helped spur new investment activity and consumer spending, eventually leading Japan back onto a path toward recovery.

392. **Some of the reforms implemented during this period included liberalizing markets and reducing taxes** to create an environment conducive to foreign investment.

393. **The Lost Decade saw a large increase in public debt due to government spending on infrastructure projects,** which reached over 200 percent of the GDP by 2011 (compared to around 60 percent before 1990).

394. **Despite all these problems, some people argue that Japan benefited from its Lost Decade** since it forced the country to rethink how it did business and come up with new methods of working to compete globally.

395. **Many Japanese companies became stronger than before after this difficult period.** The need to navigate through economic hardships led to efficiency improvements, innovative business strategies, and a greater focus on global competitiveness. **These changes helped some companies become more agile,** innovative, and internationally competitive.

396. **Some prominent examples of companies that succeeded in navigating the challenges of this period are Sony and Honda,** which still hold strong positions around the world today.

397. **In the 1990s, an increased emphasis was placed on education,** with more students pursuing higher education opportunities abroad after graduating high school.

398. **As a result of the Lost Decade, many large corporations,** which had previously guaranteed employment for life with pensions, began to end these policies. This move mostly affected older workers, who made up a large portion of the homeless.

399. **Elderly people who could move in with their children did so,** marking a huge shift in Japanese culture.

400. A major event that happened in Japan in the 1990s was a terrorist attack. On March 20th, 1995, **the Aum Shinrikyo cult launched a terrorist gas attack on the Tokyo subway,** killing twenty-seven people and injuring thousands. The attacks shocked the nation and the world.

Economic Expansion
(2000–Present)

This chapter will explore the story of Japan's economic expansion from 2000 to the present. We'll look at twenty interesting facts about **Prime Minister Shinzo Abe's** "Abenomics" policy and its impact on investments in businesses.

401. In 2000, **Japan's economy was beginning to recover** from a decade-long recession, but its GDP growth rate was around 1.7 percent.

402. By 2006, **the Japanese economy had grown by over 4 percent,** with exports reaching an all-time high of $637 billion.

403. In 2009, **Japan saw a sharp decline in economic activity** due to the global financial crisis, experiencing its worst two quarters since World War II. However, it bounced back quickly in 2010 with strong export growth and increased consumer spending fueled by government stimulus measures.

404. **Beginning in 2011, Prime Minister Shinzo Abe implemented his "Abenomics" policy,** which sought to jumpstart long-term sustainable economic growth through aggressive monetary easing and fiscal reform programs.

405. As a result of this policy, in 2010, **Japan's GDP increased almost 10 percent over the prior year.**

406. **In 2020, Tokyo hosted the Summer Olympics,** which provided a major boost to tourism and investments in local businesses.

407. In 2015, **Japan's economy experienced a brief period of deflation as prices dropped due to lower oil and commodity costs.** However, this was quickly reversed in 2016 when inflation returned to positive territory for the first time since 2013.

408. In 2018, **Prime Minister Shinzo Abe's government raised the national sales tax from 8 percent to 10 percent.** This hurt consumption but helped reduce public debt levels.

409. **In Japan, female workforce participation has increased in the past twenty years.** Women now make up about 50 percent of all workers. A much smaller percentage hold managerial positions.

410. **In Japan, in 2021, exports have grown by over 6 percent to $911 billion since 1991.**

411. **Japan has become a leader in developing innovative technologies such as robotics, artificial intelligence (AI), and autonomous vehicles.** Its government is investing heavily in research and development to ensure that the country stays ahead of the curve when it comes to innovation.

412. **One problem facing Japan is the aging of its workforce.** The Japanese birthrate has been dropping for decades, and the workforce is older, prompting some to call for the easing of immigration restrictions. More conservative people believe this will weaken Japan's unique culture.

413. **Japan has managed to keep inflation under control even in the aftermath of the COVID pandemic, unlike other nations like the US,** which have experienced increases in the inflation rate.

414. **The Japanese yen is a strong currency in Asia with a stable exchange rate,** allowing for domestic stability and international investments in Japan.

415. **Japan is the world's third-largest economy** as of 2023) and has consistently maintained a high level of economic growth since 2000. **This has enabled Japan to become an increasingly important global player in terms of trade, finance, and diplomacy.** (This figure does not include the EU but counts individual European countries.)

416. **Japanese companies have been growing around the world,** operating in over one hundred countries and creating jobs abroad while increasing the standard of living and income in Japan.

417. **Japanese technology and engineering expertise make it an appealing place to invest in infrastructure projects like bridges, roads, and ports,** which help economic growth both at home and around the world.

418. **One concern for the Japanese economy is the increased budget for the Japanese military,** which has been on the rise in the last few years as tensions with China over disputed islands and ocean territories increase.

419. Since 2020, **Japan has established several free-trade agreements (FTAs) with key trading partners such as the United States, Canada, and China.** This has allowed for tariff-free imports of goods, which helps support businesses in Japan and abroad.

420. **Shinzo Abe stepped down as prime minister in 2020 but remained a power in Japanese politics.** He was killed by an assassin on July 8th, 2022, while campaigning for a political ally.

International Relations
(2000–Present)

Japan's international relations have become increasingly complex and multifaceted over the years. This chapter will explore twenty interesting facts about the nation's relationship with countries like North Korea, South Korea, China, the United States of America, India, and Russia.

421. **In 2000, Japan and North Korea signed the Pyongyang Declaration,** which committed both countries to strive for peaceful relations. However, since that time, **North Korea has developed nuclear weapons** and advanced missile technology that can threaten Japan. Relations between the two nations in 2023 are not very good.

422. In 2002, **Prime Minister Koizumi of Japan visited China to improve Sino-Japanese relations.** This was a big step in the foreign policies of both countries, but since that time, relations between the two countries have soured.

423. In 2004, **a summit was held between South Korea and Japan that resulted in both nations agreeing on several issues,** such as education exchanges, cultural cooperation projects, and economic collaboration initiatives.

424. **Japan is still treated with suspicion in South Korea,** which suffered greatly during the Japanese occupation (1910–1945).

425. **One of the major issues between Japan and Korea has to do with the sexual slavery of Korean women by Japanese troops during WWII,** which is also an issue with China.

426. **In 2008, Japan's prime minister, Taro Aso, took steps to improve relationships with Asian countries.** He even attempted peace talks peace with North Korea despite other nations like the US and South Korea disagreeing.

427. **The year 2010 marked the first visit of a Chinese president, Hu Jintao, to Japan,** a significant step in improving ties between the two nations.

428. Since 2021, **Japan has begun increasing the size and effectiveness of its military in response to regional threats.**

429. **Prime Minister Naoto Kan resigned in 2011, and a new prime minister, Yoshihiko Noda,** tried to improve Japan's relations with China through talks about the contested Senkaku Islands. In 2024, the islands are still a point of contention between the two nations. **They are known as the Diaoyu Islands in China.**

430. **The year 2012 saw Chinese President Xi Jinping visit Tokyo.** This meeting was aimed at strengthening the Sino-Japanese bilateral relationship by signing agreements regarding trade, energy cooperation, and cultural exchanges.

431. **The year 2014 brought about another change of leadership after Shinzo Abe won the election,** making him prime minister again after a five-year hiatus. He vowed to strengthen Japan's security and international relations.

432. **In 2015, the US pressured Japan to begin to change its policy of not sending its military overseas,** as increased US commitments around the world were taking a toll.

433. In 2016, **Indian Prime Minister Narendra Modi visited Tokyo.** Both countries made agreements on economic matters, like investing $35 billion in science and technology over the course of five years.

434. **The year 2017 marked the sixtieth anniversary of diplomatic ties between South Korea and Japan.** Much effort was put into improving bilateral relations, which resulted in an agreement about the comfort women issue during that year's summit. (The comfort women were women seized from Korea and other nations during WWII and forced to become sexual objects for the use of Japanese troops.)

435. **The year 2018 was marked by Shinzo Abe's visit to China,** which was aimed at promoting better understanding between the two nations through increased trade collaboration and development projects.

436. **To this day, many Asian countries get upset when Japanese prime ministers visit the Yasukuni Shrine in Tokyo, a war memorial.** Many convicted and accused war criminals are entombed there, so honoring them with an official visit insults many of Japan's neighbors.

437. **In 2020, Shinzo Abe had to leave his position as prime minister due to health problems. Abe had tried to build better relationships with South Korea and China.** In 2022, Abe was assassinated by a disturbed man who blamed the former prime minister for his mother's death.

438. **In 2021, Joe Biden was elected president of the United States.** He held a summit with the Japanese leader to talk about trade agreements, containing North Korea, and reducing carbon emissions.

439. **In August 2023, US President Biden hosted the leaders of Japan and South Korea at Camp David for days of talks,** mostly about growing threats from China and North Korea.

440. In 2022 and 2023, **Japan embarked on a large defense build-up to counter Chinese influence and strength in the Far East.** This was the largest Japanese defense build-up since before WWII.

Cultural Changes
(2000–Present)

Discover the amazing journey of cultural changes in Japan from 2000 to 2023 with this chapter. These twenty interesting facts will shed light on how Japanese society has transformed since the 2000s.

441. **In 2000, Japan started to become more open to foreign workers** and began importing more goods from other countries.

442. **Throughout the 1990s and early 2000s, internet use and infrastructure spread in Japan,** first in the large cities and then in the rest of the country.

443. In 2004, **a new law was passed allowing women to keep their family name after marriage** instead of taking their husband's name.

444. **Japanese music has been influenced by different international styles,** such as hip-hop, rock, and EDM (electronic dance music).

445. Starting around 2006, **there was an increase in eating out at restaurants** rather than cooking meals at home due to busy lifestyles among young adults.

446. **Even though fashion trends have been heavily influenced by Western culture,** resulting in a more casual approach to dress, Japan has a unique high-fashion culture. **Kawaii culture** ("cute" culture) **is a Japanese trend with a bit of Western influence thrown in.**

447. **By 2009, mobile phones had become an important tool for communication,** with texting and social media apps being very popular.

448. **From 2010 on, there has been an increase in people living alone due to young adults taking longer to get married or start families than previous generations.**

449. **A number of young adults still live with their parents since housing prices are very high in Japan.**

450. In 2012, **Japan began legalizing same-sex partnerships in certain cities,** making it easier for LGBTQ+ couples to gain legal recognition of their relationships. However, as of 2023, **same-sex marriage is not recognized,** and same-sex couples do not enjoy most of the legal and financial protections that "traditional" couples do.

451. Since 2013, **Japanese culture has seen a small increase in embracing diversity, with TV shows featuring racially diverse casts becoming more common.** It's important to remember that around 98 percent of Japan's population of 126 million people is ethnic Japanese.

452. **Many traditional festivals have gone through changes,** such as the introduction of LED lights alongside more traditional decorations during New Year's celebrations.

453. In 2014, **Pokémon Go was released, leading to increased interest in augmented reality gaming,** as well as an increase in people going outside to explore their cities.

454. **Many Japanese are still interested in traditional crafts, such as calligraphy, origami, and pottery.** Both older and younger generations enjoy these crafts.

455. In 2011, **Japan experienced the Tohoku earthquake and tsunami, which caused massive devastation to the city of Sendai and the surrounding area.** Additionally, the quake caused a massive tsunami that killed thousands.

456. **The quake and the tidal wave caused a failure in the Fukushima Daichi Nuclear Power Plant** and spread deadly levels of radiation throughout the region, which has been largely closed off since.

457. **The quake and tsunami cost billions, took twenty thousand lives,** and sparked a debate over nuclear power in Japan that continues today.

458. **In the last decade, there has been more emphasis on mental health awareness,** with initiatives such as **Mental Health Day** being introduced in schools and workplaces.

459. **Burnout is very prominent among urban professionals,** who, because of cultural expectations, literally work themselves to an early death or suicide.

460. **In Japan, there is still a wide pay gap between men and women,** though efforts to change this have increased in recent years.

461. **Since the early 2000s, more and more Japanese baseball players are succeeding in American baseball.** They are getting a larger and larger fan base as the years pass.

462. **In June 2023, a law promoting understanding of LGBTQ+ people was passed, but it does not directly prohibit discrimination.** It encourages government entities, businesses, and schools to strive for understanding and avoid unfair discrimination, but it lacks concrete enforcement mechanisms.

463. **The latest trend is toward eco-friendly living practices. Japan has seen an increase in sustainable habits among consumers,** including reducing waste through recycling, reusing, and composting.

464. **Japan committed to combating climate change by joining the Paris Agreement in 2016,** which seeks to reduce greenhouse gas emissions.

465. As of 2024, **Tokyo's population is estimated to be around thirty-seven million,** making it one of the most populous cities in the world. It is also one of the most densely populated cities on Earth, with more than six thousand people per square kilometer.

Japanese Entertainment

Since the late 1950s, **Japanese movies and, later, TV shows and animation have had a huge impact worldwide.** From Godzilla to the amazing popularity of anime, people around the world have gotten to know more about Japanese culture. Here is a list of fifteen important milestones in Japanese entertainment history since the 1950s.

466. **Rashomon** (1950): **Directed by Akira Kurosawa,** this film introduced the concept of unreliable narration to global cinema.

467. **Seven Samurai** (1954): **Another Akira Kurosawa masterpiece,** this epic samurai film has influenced countless Western films, such as The Magnificent Seven.

468. **Godzilla** (1954): **The original kaiju film directed by Ishiro Honda** introduced the world to the iconic monster and spawned a long-running franchise.

469. **Iron Chef** (1993–1999): **This cooking competition show** gained a cult following and inspired spin-offs and adaptations worldwide.

470. **Neon Genesis Evangelion** (1995–1996): **An anime series that redefined the mecha genre and explored psychological and philosophical themes.**

471. **Pokémon** (1997–present): **The global phenomenon that started as an anime series** and expanded into video games, trading cards, and more.

472. **Battle Royale** (2000): **A controversial film that inspired the Hunger Games,** exploring the concept of children forced into deadly games.

473. **Spirited Away** (2001**): A critically acclaimed anime film by Hayao Miyazaki** that won an Academy Award, bringing Japanese animation to international attention.

474. **Terrace House** (2012–2020): **A reality TV show that offers a unique glimpse into Japanese culture and social dynamics.**

475. **Attack on Titan** (2013–2021): A modern anime series that gained international popularity for its intense storytelling and animation.

476. **Akira Kurosawa** (1910–1998): **A pioneering Japanese filmmaker who directed a wide range of influential films.** His works often explored themes of human nature and morality. Kurosawa's films have had a profound impact on global cinema, influencing directors like George Lucas and Martin Scorsese.

477. **Toshiro Mifune** (1920–1997): An acclaimed Japanese actor known for his collaborations with director **Akira Kurosawa**. His dynamic performances in films like **Seven Samurai and Yojimbo helped popularize samurai cinema worldwide.** Mifune was respected by other actors, directors, and critics worldwide and starred in the American mini-series Shogun, based on the best-selling book, in 1980.

478. In 2003, **Tom Cruise starred in The Last Samurai, which is based on a true story that took place during the Meiji Restoration** (though the hero in real life was French, not American).

479. **In 2024, the FX channel streamed a reboot of Shogun,** which is told more from a Japanese perspective than the previous mini-series. It is one of the most expensive mini-series ever made and took nearly ten years to be made.

480. In 2021, **Godzilla faced off against King Kong in the movie Godzilla vs. King Kong.** It was such a hit that a sequel is scheduled for release in 2024.

Japanese Celebrities

Like the United States, Japan has a celebrity culture. Tabloids, social media, TV programs, and more inform the public of the accomplishments and lives of their favorite media celebrities and sports stars. Here are some of the most well-known movie, TV, and sports stars in recent years in Japan.

481. **Hidetoshi Nakata is a renowned soccer player who gained fame for his exceptional midfield skills.** He played for several top European clubs and represented Japan in multiple World Cups.

482. **Ichiro Suzuki made a significant impact in both Japanese and Major League Baseball.** He was known for his exceptional batting, speed, and fielding abilities, earning numerous accolades and records.

483. **Hikaru Utada is a prominent singer-songwriter who achieved widespread fame with her J-pop and R&B music.** Her albums became bestsellers, and she's recognized as one of Japan's most successful musical artists. Some may recognize her work in the Kingdom Hearts video game series.

484. **Takeshi Kitano, also known as "Beat Takeshi," is a multi-talented figure.** He's a comedian, actor, filmmaker, and artist known for his unique brand of humor and internationally acclaimed films.

485. **Kazushi Sakuraba gained fame as a mixed martial artist and professional wrestler.** He became a legend in **Japan's PRIDE Fighting Championships** and is known for his innovative fighting style and memorable bouts.

486. **Yoko Shimomura is a renowned composer in the video game industry.** She's famous for creating memorable soundtracks for games like the Kingdom Hearts series and Final Fantasy XV.

487. **Shigeru Miyamoto is a legendary video game designer and creator of iconic franchises like Super Mario,** The Legend of Zelda, and Donkey Kong. His work revolutionized the gaming industry.

488. **Naomi Kawase gained international recognition for her unique and personal filmmaking style.** She's known for exploring themes of family, nature, and human connections in her films.

489. **Ayumi Hamasaki is a pop icon often referred to as the "Empress of J-pop."** She achieved immense success with her music. She has numerous chart-topping singles and a dedicated fanbase.

490. Kohei Uchimura is a celebrated artistic gymnast who dominated the sport during his career. He has won multiple Olympic and World Championship gold medals and showcased exceptional skills on various apparatuses.

491. **Yuzuru Hanyu is a figure skating sensation known for his technical prowess and artistic performances.** He has won multiple Olympic gold medals and set records in men's singles skating.

492. **Kosuke Kitajima is a retired swimmer renowned for his achievements in breaststroke events.** He won multiple Olympic gold medals and set world records, leaving a lasting impact on Japanese swimming.

493. **Ai Sugiyama was a top-ranked tennis player who gained recognition for her consistent performances in both singles and doubles.** She represented Japan in numerous Grand Slam tournaments.

494. **Takashi Murakami is a contemporary artist known for his vibrant and pop-inspired artwork.** He's credited with blurring the lines between high art and commercial culture.

495. **Masahiro Sakurai is a game developer and the creator of the Super Smash Bros. series.** His innovative crossover fighting games have become beloved by gamers worldwide.

496. **Ryuichi Sakamoto is a pioneering musician and composer known for his electronic and experimental music.** He's also an Academy Award-winning film composer.

497. **Koji Yakusho is a highly respected actor known for his versatile roles in Japanese cinema.** He has appeared in a wide range of films, both domestically and internationally.

498. **Hiromi Uehara, often known simply as Hiromi, is a jazz pianist and composer with a virtuosic playing style that fuses various musical influences.**

499. **Kimiko Date was a trailblazing tennis player who became Japan's first female player to reach the top five in the Women's Tennis Association singles rankings,** inspiring a new generation of tennis players.

500. **Takanohana Koji was a sumo wrestler who achieved the prestigious title of yokozuna.** He was known for his dominant performances and contributions to the sport's popularity.

Conclusion

This book has explored Japan's history from its prehistoric origins up to the present day. Along the way, we have seen **how different dynasties and eras** shaped Japanese society as it exists today.

From **the Yayoi period's** introduction of wet-rice cultivation to **the Meiji Restoration** that opened Japan to Western-style democracy, each period brought with it unique economic, cultural, political, and international changes.

Learning about history allows us to learn more about the world as it exists today. We encourage you to check out our sources page to learn even more about **Japanese history.**

If you enjoyed this book, a review on Amazon would be greatly appreciated because it would mean a lot to hear from you.

To leave a review:

1. Open your camera app.
2. Point your mobile device at the QR code.
3. The review page will appear in your web browser.

Thanks for your support!

Check out another book in the series

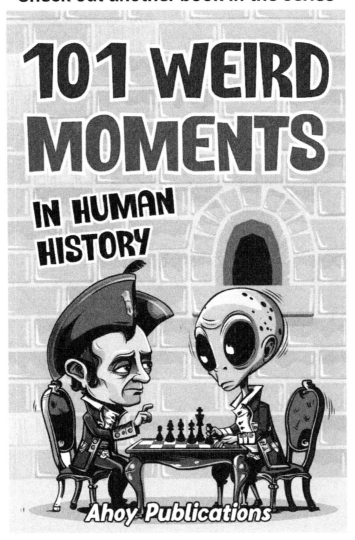

Welcome Aboard, Check Out This Limited-Time Free Bonus!

Ahoy, reader! Welcome to the Ahoy Publications family, and thanks for snagging a copy of this book! Since you've chosen to join us on this journey, we'd like to offer you something special.

Check out the link below for a FREE e-book filled with delightful facts about American History.

But that's not all - you'll also have access to our exclusive email list with even more free e-books and insider knowledge. Well, what are ye waiting for? Click the link below to join and set sail toward exciting adventures in American History.

Access your bonus here: https://ahoypublications.com/

Or, Scan the QR code!

Sources and Additional References

"Zhou Dynasty Rulers." History Today, www.historytoday.com/zhoudynastyrulers/316517, Accessed October 26 2020.

"Social Structure in Ancient China," World History Encyclopedia, https://www.worldhistory.encyclopedia.com/socialstructure/ancient/china/html, Accessed October 26 2020.

The Editors of Encyclopedia Britannica. "Pre-Imperial China." Encyclopedia Britannica, Encyclopedia Britannica, Inc., 24 June 2019, www.britannica.com/topic/pre-imperial-China#ref863156.

Smith, Mark J., ed. "Confucius." Ancient History Encyclopedia 05 Aug 2012: n pag Web 09 September 2020 https://www.ancienthistoryencyclopedia.

"Writing." Ancient China for Kids, The Oriental Institute of the University of Chicago, https://oi.uchicago.edu/research/learn-about-ancient-china/life-ancient-china/writing/.

Gannett, Rachel. "Ancient Chinese Astronomy and Mathematics: Astrolabes and Tally Sticks – Ancient History Encyclopedia." Ancient History Encyclopedia, 28 July 2017, https://www.ancient.eu/article/1082/.

"Great Wall of China: Construction & Building of the Great Wall – HISTORY." HISTORY, A&E Television Networks, 13 Dec 2019, https://www.history.com/topics/great-wall-of-china/great-wall-of-china#:~:text=The%20construction%20and%20repair%20of,by%201025).

"Early Preimperial China". The Metropolitan Museum of Art, https ://www.metmuseum.org/toah/hd/epc_3/hd_epc_3.htm (accessed April 10th 2020).

"The Invention of Paper." Science Museum, https://www.sciencemuseumgroup.org/articles/the-invention-of-paper/.

Sun Tzu, and Thomas Cleary (trans.). The Art of War: Translation and Commentary by Thomas Cleary / Sun Tzu; Foreword by John Minford; Afterword & Notes on Sources by Roger Ames / Shambhala Classics., Shambhala Publications [distributor], 2016.

"The I Ching or Book of Changes" The Internet Sacred Text Archive Home Page, sacredtextsarchiveorg/.

"Agricultural Production in Ancient China: The Great Inventions." Ancient History Encyclopedia, 27 Mar. 2020, www.ancient.eu/article/1401/.

"Qin Shi Huang: The First Emperor." History, A&E Television Networks, 2020, www.history.com/topics/ancient-history/qin-shi-huang#section_5.

"The Han Dynasty." Ancient History Encyclopedia, 19 Feb. 2019, www.ancient.eu/Han_Dynasty/.

Kallen, Stuart A. "The Han Dynasty." Encyclopedia Britannica, https://www.britannica.com/topic/Han-dynasty-Chinese-history. Accessed 27 June

2020.

Lewis, Mark Edward. *The Early Chinese Empires: Qin and Han*. Harvard University Press, 2007.

"The Great Wall of China | Overview & Facts | Britannica" Encyclopedia Britannica, Encyclopedia Britannica Inc., 23 June 2020, www.britannica.com/topic/Great -Wall -of - China.

Qian, Sima. *The Records of the Grand Historian*. Columbia University Press, 1974.

Cao, Biography.com Editors. "Cao Cao." Biography. A&E Television Networks, 2018.

Liu Bei biography: Liu Bei – Ancient History Encyclopedia https://www.ancienthistoryencyclopediaorg/liu-bei/(Accessed 14 June 2020).

"Jin Dynasty (265–420)." Encyclopedia Britannica; accessed June 20th 2021; https://www.britannica.com/topic/Jin-dynasty-Chinese-history.

"The Warring States Period," Ancient China, accessed June 8, 2021, https://www.ancient.eu/Warring_States_Period/.

"Sixteen Kingdoms." Britannica, The Editors of Encyclopedia Britannica, https://www.britannica.com/topic/Sixteen-Kingdoms.

"The Period of Northern and Southern Dynasties (420-589 CE)." Ancient History Encyclopedia, Ancient History Encyclopedia, 7 July 2017, www.ancient.eu/Northern_and_Southern_Dynasties/.

Turner Jr., William C. "Sui Dynasty (589–618 CE)." Khan Academy, Khan Academy, khanacademy.org/humanities/world-history/ancient-medieval/sui--tang--song-dynasties-(400ce---1200ce)/v/the--sui—dynasty.

"Grand Canal (China)." Encyclopedia Britannica, Encyclopedia Britannica, Inc., 23 Apr 2021, https://www.britannica.com/topic/Grand-Canal-China#ref406020

"Sui Dynasty (581–618)." Encyclopedia Britannica, https://www.britannica.com/topic/Sui-dynasty. Accessed 27 Apr 2021.

"The Tang Dynasty (618–907 CE)." Ancient History Encyclopedia, ancient.eu/Tang_Dynasty/.

"Women in the Tang Dynasty." Asia Society Museum Education Center for Arts & Culture, asiasocietymuseumedcenterforartscultureedu/womeninthetanddynasty. Accessed 18 Nov 2020.

Shaughnessy, Edward L., ed. *The Cambridge History of Ancient China: From the Origins of Civilization to 221 B.C.* Cambridge University Press, 1999.

Murphey, Rhoads. "Eunuchs and Power in Ming China" University of South Carolina Press, 2009-.www.uscpressedusccmceunuch.html>.

"The Five Dynasties and Ten Kingdoms Period." Ancient History Encyclopedia, ancient.eu/five_dynasties_and_ten_kingdoms/.

"Western Xia Dynasty | Chinese History | Britannica." Encyclopedia Britannica, www.britannica.com/place/Western-Xia-dynasty#ref1060483/.

"History of Acupuncture." Healthline Media UK Ltd., 2019, healthline.com/health/history – ofacupuncture.

"Liao Dynasty." Encyclopedia Britannica, Encyclopedia Britannica, Inc., 15 Apr. 2020, www.britannica.com/topic/Liao-Dynasty#ref879107.

Ebrey, Patricia Buckley. *The Cambridge Illustrated History of China* (Cambridge Illustrated Histories). Cambridge University Press; 2 edition (August 30, 1999).

"Song Dynasty." Encyclopedia Britannica, www.britannica.com/topic/Song-dynasty.

"Genghis Khan and the Mongol Conquest of China - Asia for Educators - Columbia University." Accessed May 8, 2021. https://afe.easia.columbia.edu/mongols/pop_genghisconquestchinapowerpointlessonplan2_.htm

"Silk Road," National Geographic, https://www.nationalgeographic.org/topics/exploration-and-adventure/silk-road/.

"Yuan Dynasty." Ancient History Encyclopedia, ancient.eu/yuan_dynasty/.

"Kublai Khan." Encyclopedia Britannica, www.britannica.com/biography/Kublai-Khan.

"The Travels of Marco Polo." The British Library, www.bl.uk/collectionitems/the-travels-of-marco-polo.

"Ming Dynasty." Encyclopedia Britannica, https://www.britannica.com/topic/Ming-dynasty#ref83635.

"Qing Dynasty (1644–1911)." Encyclopedia Britannica, Encyclopedia Britannica, Inc., https://www.britannica.com/place/Qing-dynasty.

Beasley, William G. "Manchu People" Encyclopedia Britannica, Encyclopedia Britannica, Inc., 8 Oct 2012, https://www.britannica.com/topic/Manchu-people#ref630815.

"Sino-European Trade". Asian Art Museum, Asian Art Museum San Francisco, http://www.asianartmuseum.org/documents/lessonplan_chinatrade.pdf

"Emperor Tongzhi." Encyclopedia Britannica, https://www.britannica.com/biography/Tongzhi-emperor-of-China. Accessed 7 Apr 2021

"Empress Cixi of China." Biography, A&E Television Networks LLC., 29 October 2016, https://www.biography.com/royalty/empress-cixi-of-china Accessed 7 April 2021.

"The Opium War (1839-1842)." History, www.history.com/topics/opium-wars/.

Hanes III, W Travis and Frank Sanello. *The Opium Wars: The Addiction of One Empire and the Corruption of Another*. Sourcebooks Trade Paperback Edition (October 1st 2002).

MacGillivray, Donald. "The Tongzhi Restoration (1862-1908)." Encyclopedia Britannica, 16 Apr. 2021, www.britannica.com/topic/Tongzhi-restoration.

"The Boxer Rebellion." History.com, A&E Television Networks, 2020, www.history.com/topics/19th-century/boxer-rebellion#:~:text=In%20late%201900s%20China,overthrow%20foreigners'ruleinChina.

Belenky, Alexander M., and Mark Czarnecki, eds. *The Chinese Revolution of 1911: A Brief History with Documents*, Bedford St Martin's (2017).

"Republican Revolution in China," Encyclopedia Britannica Online Academic Edition, accessed March 6 2021 https://www.britannica.com/event/Republican-Revolution#ref495887.

"Kuomintang." Encyclopedia Britannica, https://www.britannica.com/topic/Kuomintang-Nationalist-Party-of-China#ref302070.

"Chinese Civil War." Encyclopedia Britannica, Encyclopedia Britannica, Inc., 10 Mar. 2021, https://www.britannica.com/event/Chinese-Civil-War.

"Chiang Kai Shek and the Nationalists in China | Asia for Educators | Columbia University." Accessed 11 March 2021 http://afe.easia.columbia.edu/special/china_1900_chiangkaishek.htm.

"The People's Republic of China." The World Factbook, Central Intelligence Agency, 2019, www.cia.gov/library/publications/the-world-factbook/geos/ch.html

"The Cultural Revolution: Political Campaign Launched by Mao Zedong 1966–1976." The Cultural Revolution: Political Campaign Launched by Mao Zedong 1966–1976 | Britannica, www.britannica.com/event/Cultural-Revolution#ref351884.

"Tiananmen Square Protests." History.com, A&E Television Networks, 2 Nov. 2009, www.history.com/topics/tiananmen-square-protests.

May, Julian. The Prehistory of Japan. Routledge, 2019.

Takakia, Kazuo. Prehistoric Japan: New Perspectives on Insular East Asia. U of Hawaii P, 2008.

Miller, Laura. Religions in Japan: Buddhism, Shinto, Christianity. Japan Society, 1989.

Brown, Delmer M., and Ichirō Ishida, eds. The Cambridge History of Japan. Vol. 1, Ancient Japan. The Cambridge UP, 1993.

Qiu, Jenny. "Yayoi Period." Encyclopedia Britannica, Encyclopedia Britannica, Inc., 9 Feb. 2018, www.britannica.com/topic/Yayoi-period.

Chisholm, Kate. "Kofun period." Encyclopedia Britannica. September 08 2020. https://www.britannica.com/event/Kofun-period-Japanese-history.

"Seventeen Article Constitution." Encyclopedia Britannica, Encyclopedia Britannica, Inc., 16 Jul. 2015, https://www.britannica.com/topic/Seventeen-Article-Constitution.

"Asuka Period." Arts, Encyclopedia Britannica, https://www.britannica.com/ topic/Asuka-period.

"The Nara Period." Encyclopedia Britannica, https://www.britannica.com /event/Nara-period.

Hayashi, Miki. "Heian Period (794-1185): Japanese History and Culture." Britannica.com, The Encyclopedia Britannica, Inc., 28 Aug. 2020, www.britannica.com/topic/Heian-period.

"Noh Theater." Encyclopedia Britannica, www.britannica.com/art/Noh-theater.

"Kamakura Period." Encyclopedia Britannica, www.britannica.com/topic/ Kamakura-period.

Tsuzi, Atta. History of Japan. Infobase Publishing, 2007.

Carrington, Hereward. Historical and Cultural Atlas of Japan. Facts on File, 2007.

Plath, David W. Japanese Society at the Turn of the Century. University of California Press, 1995.

Kakutani, Michio. Zen Culture. Vintage Books, 1980.

Ushio, Shinobu. Japanese Culture. A Short History. Routledge, 2014.

Gordon, Andrew. "Tokugawa Japan." Encyclopedia Britannica, Encyclopedia Britannica, Inc., www.britannica.com/place/Japan/Tokugawa-Japan-1603-1868.

Gordon, Andrew. "Sakoku." Encyclopedia Britannica, Encyclopedia Britannica, Inc., www.britannica.com/topic/sakoku.

"Kabuki, Traditional Theatre of Japan." Encyclopedia Britannica, Encyclopedia Britannica, Inc., www.britannica.com/art/kabuki.

Gordon, Andrew. "Tokugawa Japan." Encyclopedia Britannica, Encyclopedia Britannica, Inc., www.britannica.com/place/Japan/Tokugawa-Japan-1603-1868.

"Meiji Restoration," World History Encyclopedia, Dec. 2017, https://www.worldhistory.org/Meiji_Restoration/.

"Meiji Period: Economic Development," Encyclopedia Britannica, https://www.britannica.com/place/Japan/Meiji-period-1868-1912-economic-development.

"First Sino-Japanese War (1894–95)," Encyclopedia Britannica, https://www.britannica.com/event/First-Sino-Japanese-War-1894-95.

"Russo-Japanese War (1904–05)," Encyclopedia Britannica, https://www.britannica.com/event/Russo-Japanese-War.

"Woman's Suffrage in Japan." Wikipedia, Wikimedia Foundation, 27 Feb. 2021, en.wikipedia.org/wiki/Women%27s_suffrage_in_Japan.

"Abenomics," Wikipedia, Wikimedia Foundation, 7 Mar. 2021, en.wikipedia.org/wiki/Abenomics.

"Meiji Constitution." Encyclopedia Britannica, Accessed 12 May 2021, https://www.britannica.com/topic/Meiji-Constitution.

"Prime Minister Junichiro Koizumi." Britannica, Encyclopedia Britannica, Inc., 21 Mar. 2018, www.britannica.com/biography/Junichiro-Koizumi.

Charles D. Anderson. "Shinzo Abe." Britannica, Encyclopedia Britannica, Inc., 22 May 2020, www.britannica.com/biography/Shinzo-Abe.

Oshiro Kanda. "Yasuo Fukuda." Britannica, Encyclopedia Britannica, Inc., 18 Dec. 2020, www.britannica.com/biography/Yasuo-Fukuda

"Yoshihiko Noda." Britannica, Encyclopedia Britannica, Inc., 18 Dec. 2020, www.britannica.com/biography/Yoshihiko-Noda.

Printed in Great Britain
by Amazon

50343673R00079